PENGUIN PASSNOTES

GCSE English

Roisin Babuta was born in London and educated at King's
College, London, St John's College, Oxford, and St Cross
College, Oxford. After completing a thesis on Charles
Dickens's treatment of death in his novels, she taught at
Oxford, at Salisbury and at the Godolphin and Latymer School
in London. She now devotes most of her time to her academic
and creative writing but retains some teaching at Godolphin and
Latymer.

PENGUIN PASSNOTES

GCSE English

ROISIN M. BABUTA, B.A.(Hons.), M.Litt.(Oxon.).
ADVISORY EDITOR: STEPHEN COOTE, M.A., PH.D.

PENGUIN BOOKS

PENGUIN BOOKS

Published by the Penguin Group
27 Wrights Lane, London W 8 5 T Z, England
Viking Penguin Inc., 40 West 23rd Street, New York, New York 10010, U S A
Penguin Books Australia Ltd, Ringwood, Victoria, Australia
Penguin Books Canada Ltd, 2801 John Street, Markham, Ontario, Canada L 3 R 1 B 4
Penguin Books (N Z) Ltd, 182–190 Wairau Road, Auckland 10, New Zealand

Penguin Books Ltd, Registered Offices: Harmondsworth, Middlesex, England

First published 1988

Filmset in Linotron Ehrhardt by
Rowland Phototypesetting Ltd, Bury St Edmunds, Suffolk
Made and printed in Great Britain by
Richard Clay Ltd, Bungay, Suffolk

Table of Contents

Acknowledgements

I am most grateful to my colleagues in the English Department of Godolphin and Latymer School for their invaluable help and advice, and also to the Headmistress, Miss Margaret Rudland, for her support.

I would also like to thank my Fourth Year Teaching Group, Group Two, 1986–7, for their enthusiastic and intelligent participation in the various exercises contained in this book. Special thanks also to Beatrice Aidin, Kate Beckinsale, Nisha Jani, Aletta Seymour, Ellen Taylor, Pola Wickham and Silole Wuensche, examples of whose work appear in the book.

Roisin Michéle Babuta
London 1987

Acknowledgements

For permission to reproduce extracts of prose or poetry, acknowledgement is made to the following:

For the article by Sir Kenneth Baker on new education proposals to *The Guardian*; for the pie chart and bar chart (BBC Annual Report and Handbook, 1987), to BBC Enterprises Ltd; for Richard Church (*Over the Bridge*), to Laurence Pollinger & Co. and the Estate of Richard Church; for *Instructions for Defrosting the Freezer*, from Collins' *Practical Dictionary of Household Hints*, to Marshall Cavendish Books Limited; for Alan Garner (*The Owl Service*), to William Collins PLC; for Graham Greene (*Brighton Rock* and *The Destructors*, from *Brighton Rock* and *Collected Stories*), to William Heinemann Ltd. & The Bodley Head, Ltd; for Susan Hill (*I'm the King of the Castle*), to Hamish Hamilton Ltd; for Ted Hughes ('The Horses', from *The Hawk in the Rain*), to Faber and Faber Ltd; for Programme Transmissions on Channel 4 and ITV (weekly averages, year ended 29th March 1987), to IBA (Annual Report & Accounts 1986–7); for Clive James (*The Crystal Bucket*), to *The Observer*; for Jeremy Kingston ('The Hobbit' at the Fortune Theatre – *The Times*, 11 December, 1986, copyright © Times Newspapers Ltd 1987; for James Kirkup 'A House in Summer', from *The Prodigal Son* – Penguin Book of Contemporary Verse, ed. Kenneth Allott, 1962), to Oxford University Press; for Philip Larkin ('Wedding Wind' from *The Less Deceived*), to Marvell Press; for Laurie Lee (*As I Walked Out One Midsummer Morning*), to André Deutsch Ltd; for Laurie Lee (*Cider with Rosie*), to The Hogarth Press; for Talybont Reservoir (*The Macmillan Guide to Britain's Nature Reserves*), to Macmillan London Ltd; for Olivia Manning (*The Rain Forest*), to William Heinemann Ltd; for Arthur Miller (*Death of a Salesman*, copyright © Arthur Miller 1949), to Elaine Greene Ltd; for R. K. Narayan (*A Tiger for Malgudi*), to William Heinemann Ltd; for George Orwell (*Christmas*), to A. M. Heath & Company Limited, the Estate of the late Sonia Brownell Orwell and Secker & Warburg Limited; for George Orwell ('The Sporting Spirit'), to A. M. Heath & Company Limited, for John Osborne (*Look Back in Anger*), to Faber and Faber Ltd; for Theodore Roethke ('The Meadow Mouse', from *The Collected Poems of Theodore Roethke*), to Faber and Faber Ltd; for 'Sixth Formers Learn about Aids', from *The Sunday Times*, 15th March, 1987, to *The Sunday Times*; for William Trevor (*The Children of Dynmouth*), to The Bodley Head; for Virginia Woolf (*The Years* and *To the Lighthouse*), to the author's Literary Estate and The Hogarth Press.

Introduction

In your GCSE English examination, you will have to prove that you can use language effectively for a variety of purposes, orally and in writing. You will be expected to be able to express your feelings accurately and sensitively; to put forward your opinions clearly and forcefully; and to organize and present facts logically and clearly. You will also need to be able to understand what other people have said and written, and why they have expressed themselves in a particular way.

You have been doing both these things for a long time already. We are all engaged throughout our lives in a constant process of observing and understanding what goes on around us. Every day, too, we are called upon to express ourselves, orally or on paper. So, when you begin your GCSE English course, you are not doing anything new. It is a matter of adjusting and perfecting the skills you already have, not of learning something from scratch. The examination is intended to test how successful you have become at using and understanding language and to provide an objective assessment of your abilities.

To do this, the GCSE English examiners will look at your success in three main areas: writing, reading and understanding, and speaking. You will be required to demonstrate your abilities through your coursework during the two years and possibly in a final examination. You will need to aim at being versatile: at being able to write, read and speak effectively, rather than being particularly good in one area.

You may know that there are five examining groups in England and Wales and they have all developed slightly different GCSE English examinations, although they all have the same aims in mind. For each, you will all have to show your ability to express yourself in writing, to read and understand and to talk in a variety of situations, but the ways in which these skills will be tested will vary from group to group. Your teacher will have selected the most suitable examination for your class and you should make sure that you know which group's examination you are sitting.

Then, you can find out exactly what you have to do to demonstrate your skills in all the different areas. You should make sure that you know the answers to the following questions:

1. Will I be sitting an examination? How high a percentage will each section of the examination count for?
2. How many pieces of coursework do I have to put in my folder?
3. Has the examining group asked for any particular types of writing to be put in the folder?

If you are not sure of any of these facts, check with your teacher so that you know exactly what you are working towards. The list below gives a bare outline of the different requirements of the groups. This should help you, but you must fill in the details with your teacher's help.

Midland Examining Group (MEG)

	Title	Duration	Weighting
Scheme 1	Paper 1 (Aural)	1¼ hours	20%
	Paper 2 (Directed Writing and Continuous Writing)	1¾ hours	50%
	Paper 3 (Coursework)	—	30%
Scheme 2	Paper 1	1¼ hours	20%
	Coursework	—	80%
Scheme 3	Coursework	—	100%

Southern Examining Group

Syllabus A   *Paper 1*
Understanding and response to literary material and directed writing: 1½ hours   25%

Paper 2
Understanding and response to non-literary material and directed writing: 1½ hours   25%

Paper 3
Coursework   50%

Syllabus B   Coursework   100%

London and East Anglian Group

either

Paper 1   Coursework   50%

and Paper 2   Understanding and response

2¼ hours   50%

or

Paper 1   Coursework (Understanding and response)   50%

and Paper 3   Coursework   50%

Northern Examining Association

Syllabus A   Written Paper (Understanding and Response and Expression)

2 hours   50%

Coursework   50%

Syllabus B   Coursework   100%

Welsh Joint Education Committee

either

Paper 1   Understanding and Response and Expression

2½ hours   50%

and Paper 2   Expressive and Factual Writing

1½ hours   30%

and Coursework B   20%

or

Paper 1   Understanding and Response and Expression

2½ hours   50%

and Coursework A   50%

For details of specific Coursework requirements, see pp. 134–44.

It is obvious that there are many different skills involved in what we call 'English' and we all have our strengths and weaknesses. Some of you will be able to write excellent stories; others will have a real talent for producing clear, accurate instructions; some will find that they can move and persuade people when they are speaking to them about their favourite topic; others will be good at keeping a cool head when faced with a difficult piece of writing. There are also quite a few people who do all these things well.

Your English course should be helping you to discover and develop your own individual talents as a reader, writer and speaker. It should also help you to become aware of your weaknesses, and to do something about those, too. Whatever course you are taking, you will be expected to show your ability to write, read and talk. So, for convenience, this book will treat those three skills separately, although they are very closely related in practice. We'll begin with writing.

1. Writing English

You will spend a great deal of time during your course writing what the examiners call 'continuous prose'. This loose term covers all kinds of different writing: short stories; descriptive or autobiographical essays; discussion essays; speeches; letters; magazine articles; reviews; reports; explanations and instructions. Some of the pieces of work you do over the two years will go into your coursework folder (for help on how to put your folder together see pp. 134–44); and other pieces you will write in the examination itself, if you are taking one, or maybe under timed conditions in class. The length of the pieces will vary, according to their purposes.

The possibilities for writing continuous prose are, as you can see, almost endless. Don't make the mistake of thinking that you have to demonstrate your abilities in *all* these forms of writing in your folder or in the examination. What you choose to write to demonstrate your skills depends a great deal on you, as long as you keep within the framework provided by your particular examining group.

WHAT CAN I WRITE?   *Expressive / Factual*

We'll now take a brief look at all the kinds of writing which could be called 'continuous prose'. Let's think of writing under two main headings: Expressive and Factual. As you can probably guess, expressive writing is the kind of personal, creative writing you do when you tell a story, invent characters or scenes, describe a place imaginatively, or recount an event in your life. In other words, you use your imagination in such essays. Factual writing is exactly what it sounds like. It is writing which deals primarily with facts and practical issues. In many ways, this type of writing is the most crucial for everyday life. It is the most disciplined and logical form of writing and the skills to be mastered here are absolutely essential for whatever job you eventually find yourself doing. Of course, you can deal with facts imaginatively. This is the sort of writing you do when composing a letter of complaint or presenting your opinions, perhaps in the form of a newspaper or magazine article or review. I have called this category 'Persuasive Writing and Journalism'. Obviously, if you have ambitions to work in radio, TV, publishing or advertising, you should pay particular attention to this area.

EXPRESSIVE WRITING

We have defined Expressive Writing as personal, creative writing. Now, let's look at different kinds of expressive writing in detail.

Narrative Essays: Short Stories

You are given a title, such as 'Daylight Robbery' or 'The Journey', and you weave a story around it, creating your own plot, characters, dialogue and settings. Those of you who enjoy telling your friends 'what happened' and take pleasure in inventing scenes and conversations will enjoy such essays.

Descriptive Essays

Your title would be something like 'The Street-Market' or 'A Place I Love'. In this kind of essay you are being asked to re-create, as vividly and originally as possible, a certain place: its sights, sounds, smells, the people you see there. You will enjoy this kind of writing if you are very observant and have a good memory.

Picture-based Essays

This kind of essay can be narrative or descriptive. You are asked to examine a picture, a photograph, a cartoon or a drawing, and to write an essay around it. Those of you who find your imaginations easily sparked off by what you *see* will do well here.

Autobiographical Essays

These are the most approachable essays of all. You are given a title such as 'My First Day at School' or 'My Parents', and you have the opportunity to rework your own experience imaginatively. Those of you who really enjoy telling slightly embroidered tales about your life and family will get on very well with this kind of essay.

PERSUASIVE WRITING AND JOURNALISM

We said that this was the kind of writing where you deal with facts imaginatively. Let's have a look at some of the possibilities in this area.

Discussion/Argumentative Essays

Your title could be 'Is Religious Education Really Necessary?', or 'Give the Case for and against Nuclear Energy'. Such essays are only to be attempted if you have a thorough knowledge of the subject, and strong views. They are especially suitable for those of you who usually win arguments through cast-iron logic!

Speeches

This is a related area. You could include in your coursework folder a copy of a speech on the kind of subject mentioned above. You may have made the speech as part of your oral English course, as long as it was not assessed formally for the examination. You will do this well if you enjoy getting up in front of an audience and persuading them over to your point of view!

Letters

You will frequently find yourself required to write letters as part of the Understanding section in the examination (see pp. 53–4). However, you could also present your feelings on a subject in an open letter to a quality newspaper for your coursework folder. Again, you need the same sort of persuasive skills as for discussion or argumentative essays and speeches.

Magazine/Newspaper Articles

This is the ideal opportunity to research a subject in which you are really interested – for example, a local building site which has become a nature reserve and is now threatened with development – and to present your ideas like a 'feature', including photographs and maps. This is an excellent coursework choice for those of you who enjoy journalistic research.

Book/Play/Film Reviews

A review is an assessment of the merits of a contemporary work and a personal response to it. It is actually *very* difficult to write a really good review – you need to be able to condense your thoughts severely and to express your feelings precisely. This is a good option for very confident writers.

FACTUAL OR PRACTICAL WRITING

You won't find yourself required to do this kind of writing on an Expression (Writing) examination paper, if you are taking one. You would be more likely to have to do it for an Understanding and Response paper. Do remember, however, that this sort of writing is also a coursework option, if you wish.

Report

A report is an account of an event or a series of events, or a summary of the conclusions to be drawn from a survey or set of statistics. It could be a summary of the findings in a survey on the eating habits of children aged twelve to fifteen, or a condensed account of the school football team's activities throughout the year. You might produce this sort of thing for the school magazine. You need to be logical and accurate and have the ability to prune your words down to a minimum (see pp. 108–9).

Explanations/Instructions

In such a piece of writing you are explaining a process or giving instructions for a process to someone who knows nothing about it. It might be the instructions for mending a puncture, for instance. You need to present every stage of the process in as logical, clear and accurate a way as possible.

Factual Descriptions

If you were asked to go and describe a part of the school for *informative* purposes, you would write a factual description. You would give a straight-forward, detailed, clear picture of what you saw, for the purpose of *informing* your readers. Your aim would be to provide a very accurate picture in your reader's mind, with none of the hazy edges you might get in a more expressive, personal description.

OTHER TYPES OF WRITING

There are also some further possibilities for more ambitious work – poetry and playscripts – which could be included in your coursework folder, but they are only for you if you are a very ambitious writer and you have arranged with your teacher to include such a piece. The talent involved will be something you have discovered yourself over the years in English lessons and in your own time. You may feel strongly that you would like to include such an assignment to demonstrate your skill and interest.

Now, let's focus in on the different types of 'continuous prose' and look at them in greater detail.

NARRATIVE ESSAYS: SHORT STORIES

A short story is in many ways like a novel in miniature. It has all the same ingredients, but there are smaller amounts of each. So, the skills you need to develop for this type of writing are very like those of a novelist.

What are those ingredients? First of all, there is the *plot* or *story-line*. This is what we call the events that happen in the story. Then there are the *characters*. They are the people who take part in these events. They have to speak, so we must write *dialogue* for them. Finally, the story must have some kind of setting, so we have a certain amount of description or *local colour*.

It stands to reason that not all of you are going to be good at all of these things. So, you should try to bring out those things you *are* good at. For instance, if you have a talent for descriptive writing, make the atmosphere of your story important. If you are particularly good at depicting characters, make the plot centre around the way they behave towards each other. There are, however, certain ways of improving your technique and considerably increasing your chances of writing such an essay well, so that you can do something about your weak areas. We'll discuss these techniques as we go along.

Where to Start

Before you even begin to write, there are a number of things you need to have clear in your mind. It is very unlikely that an essay which you begin quickly and without any planning will turn out well. So decide on:

1. The outline of the story: where it begins, what its main incidents are, and, very importantly, how it ends.
2. The people involved: have some idea of them all in your mind.
3. The setting: you should be able to visualize each stage of the story against different 'backdrops' so that you can refer briefly to where events are taking place throughout the story.
4. Your point of view: who is telling this story? Is it you, as one of the characters taking part in the story, or you as the storyteller who sees everything?

Once you have your title, the process of 'thinking up a story' need not be difficult if you remember some basic facts and are prepared to spend some time thinking. Planning your story should take you between five and ten minutes. Since the first thing to do, logically, is to work out your story-line, that is where we'll begin.

Plot

The first thing to bear in mind is that in most short stories, the simplest ideas work best. Secondly, a story does not have to be complex, sensational or shocking. But it does need to be convincing. Thirdly, your story should have only one or two main incidents and one or two main characters as it is impossible to do justice to more in such a short time. Finally, if you do discover a talent for thinking up ingenious and surprising stories – exploit it fully!

Let's think for a moment that you are sitting silently at your desk in the examination room or in class with the title 'Return Journey', and a lot of blank paper. The first thing to do is to write the title in capital letters in the middle of the page, then box it in, as shown, and let your mind wander.

RETURN JOURNEY

What we are going to do is to play a version of the 'association of ideas' game. In that game, you are given a word, then you shout out the first word that comes into your mind, and the next person carries on by doing the same. Play this game with the title. Jot down ideas, images, characters, snatches of conversation, that come into your mind. Don't be afraid to write down a whole train of thought very quickly, if it occurs to you, but also make sure that

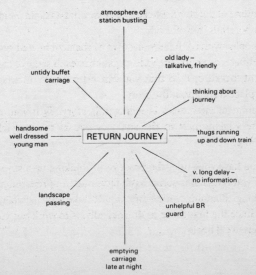

you include odd incomplete snatches of thought which have come into your mind. You will find, after two or three minutes, that you have a jigsaw puzzle of ideas and images like this.

You need to look carefully at the different jottings, keeping an open mind, and think about which ones you might be able to follow up. Which ideas appeal to you the most? Put a circle around the jottings you like the look of, cross out the ideas you don't need, then take a clean page and try to follow through the one or two ideas you have chosen. Think of a logical sequence for the events you are interested in, and ways of bringing in the characters. Begin to develop the characters more fully in your mind.

When I gave this title to my fourth year, they came up with an extraordinary range of ideas. I have picked just one possibility, worked out by one of my students using this method. She picked out from her original jottings: an old lady; an interesting young man; an unhelpful BR guard and the atmosphere of the station. These were the ideas she began with. She then developed these basic ideas, adding other thoughts on a fresh sheet of paper which became the basis of the story.

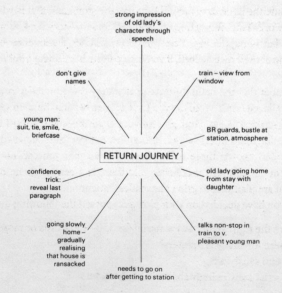

As she sorted these ideas out, a story emerged: an old lady is returning home from visiting her daughter, by train. She is friendly and talkative, and makes friends with a charming and well-dressed young man on the train. She confesses to him that she needs to make another call in London before she goes home and she does not know how she will manage with all her baggage. He offers to help: if she gives him her address and her front-door keys, he will take all her baggage home for her. She is delighted, gives him her keys, address and bags, and trots off happily to see her friend. Hours later, she returns home and is horrified to find her house burgled, and all her valuables stolen. She reports it to the police, and only at the very end of the story does she think that the young man, whom she liked, might just be responsible.

There is no doubt that this brief outline has the makings of a first-rate short story – as indeed it was. The student arrived at this very simple plot in several stages. First, she decided to focus on the old lady who went down in her original jottings. Then, she thought herself into the train carriage, imagining how her old lady would feel, speak and behave. She then opened her mind to all the things that could happen to her old lady in the train. She had put a young man in her original jottings, so she put them together and watched them talking, and he became a suave con-man before her eyes.

She made the necessary mental leap *into* the story, and that is what made this idea work. You too need to put yourself into the story, look around you, and *see* what is happening. Very often you will see a sequence of events developing of their own accord, if you concentrate hard, focus your mind and don't panic.

Remember that the main purpose of any story is to entertain: readers are very easily bored (aren't you?) so you have to keep serving them up something fresh and striking. Keep your plot moving at all times and always choose a story-line that really interests *you*. Remember to limit yourself to two or three incidents and two or three main characters, so that you can do yourself justice. You should also make sure that there is a central scene or climax where you are planning to grip your readers' attention.

Once you have decided on your plot, ask yourself the following questions:

1. Is there the right amount of material for 350–450 words or more?
2. Are there too many characters?
3. Is the end satisfying?
4. Can I write convincingly about these characters?

Think particularly carefully about question 4. Your stories will always seem more convincing and realistic if you are writing about places and people you know or are at least capable of imagining. To be specific: you will find

that you can write a far more convincing essay on what it feels like to be
bullied or to bully than you could on what it feels like to be Prime Minister.
Wherever possible, use your own experience – the ring of truth is unmistakable.

Point of View

There is just one more thing to think about before you start writing, and that
is: *who* is telling the story?

Your choice is between first- and third-person narrative. You use the
'first-person' point of view when you write as 'I': 'It was the worst party I had
ever been to. Even the dog looked bored.' You are using the 'third-person'
when you write about all the characters as 'she' or 'he': 'As far as Andrew
could see, it was the worst party he had ever been to. Even the dog looked
bored.'

There are advantages and disadvantages to both methods and you need to
learn to judge which is the most suitable viewpoint for your particular story.
To help you to decide, try to answer the following questions:

1. *Can I imagine myself in the position of the central character?* If you have ever
    been in a similar situation, or perhaps have always dreaded it, the first
    person would work well.
2. *Do I need to present the thoughts of more than one character in the story?* If your
    story depends on the reader knowing the thoughts of more than one
    character, you must use the third person. Then, you can move in and out
    of your characters' thoughts.
3. *Would the story be more effective if it looked as if the storyteller was laughing up
    his sleeve at the characters?* If you are generally taking a rather amused,
    detached view of all the characters, then the third person works best.
4. *Do the events of the story need to be seen from one person's point of view only?*
5. *Do we need to see things from one character's point of view as well as being able
    to see him or her as he or she really is?* You need to think carefully about the
    answers to both questions 4 and 5. Sometimes it is best to write from the
    first-person point of view when you intend to reveal something very
    surprising at the end, so that it comes as a shock to the characters *and* to
    the reader. You could also present the central character in a more
    detached way, so that the reader can have two ways of looking at him or

her: the character's own self-image, and the reader's more objective view.

6. *Is it important that we see the other characters in the story from another person's point of view than that of the central character?* This relates to question 2. If you need to present the thoughts of anyone other than the hero or heroine of your story, you need the third person.

7. *Is a great deal of suspense involved?*

8. *Does the plot concentrate more on actions than on feelings?* If your story depends less on character than on the working out of a tense plot, you need to be completely free to manipulate your plot, as a third-person narrator.

9. *Does the plot revolve around the emotions of one central character?* Again, it is often more convenient to present emotions directly, in the first person.

10. *Which method seems most natural?* Often your instincts will tell you which narrative method to use. The other questions are only relevant if your instincts on a particular story do not give you sufficient guidance.

To sum up: if you answered 'yes' to questions 1 and 9, the chances are the story will work better in the first person. If you answered 'yes' to questions 2, 3, 6, 7 and 8, then you would be happier with the third person. If you answered 'yes' to questions 4 and 5, then you would have a choice and would need to think especially carefully about your viewpoint.

First-person Narrative

This allows you to present directly the feelings and emotions of the central character. In a first-person narrative, every single event and every other character in the story is seen from the central character's point of view.

There are obvious advantages to this method. If you find yourself strongly sympathetic with the central character and a large part of the story will involve how he or she feels about the events of the story, this viewpoint will let you speak directly to the reader. It also lets the reader get to know the character very intimately. It is a particularly effective viewpoint for a story where something is happening which the 'I' figure does not quite understand. The reader shares the central character's feelings of unease, bafflement and suspense.

If you feel that a very personal viewpoint would be suitable for your story, there are still certain pitfalls to be avoided. The first is over-indulgence –

wallowing in the story, getting too sentimental or emotional; such stories can be very claustrophobic. You need to keep a bit of a distance between you and the 'I' character or the reader won't be able to take you seriously. Be personal, but don't just pour yourself out on paper. This point is highly relevant in the autobiographical essays, which we'll look at later.

The other pitfall is that of the viewpoint becoming blurred. This occurs when you forget that you are supposed to be writing from one person's point of view and you start talking about the feelings of other characters, describing them in a way that is not consistent with the way the hero or heroine would think or speak.

To sum up: when using the first-person narrative method:

1. Describe everything from the 'I' character's point of view.
2. Don't indulge yourself too much.
3. Let the reader experience the story *with* the central character.

Third-person Narrative

This kind of storytelling is a bit like 'playing God'! You sit in your chair and you are not confined to the thoughts of one character. You can move in and out of the minds of all your characters and you can see all the places in your story at the same time. Imagine yourself as a puppeteer, moving your characters around. The advantages of this method are obvious. You have tremendous freedom and you can present your characters and tell your story precisely in the way *you* want to, without worrying about filtering everything through one person's eyes. You can also sit back and take a detached view of all your characters.

However, if we look at all the stories we have read it does seem to be natural for a writer to focus on one central character and you may find yourself doing this, even when you have chosen to write in the third person. This is fine. The student who wrote about the old lady in the train used the third person, and with very good reason. Look at question 5 again. In a story where there is something wrong with the way a character is seeing things or people – like the way the old lady sees the suave young man – it is much better if the storyteller takes a detached view. That way, the writer encourages the reader to sit back and think, 'Hang on, she's being a bit naive, isn't she?' We can see the young man as the old lady sees him, but a part of us is thinking, 'I wouldn't trust him if I were her.' So, by all means follow one central character, but stand back a bit and think of how others may see him or her.

There are two main dangers in using this narrative method. The first is that of simply recording events and not really involving yourself in the story, so that it just becomes a string of incidents and briefly drawn characters. Try to become engaged in the story – don't just get so wrapped up in the mechanics of the plot that you lose interest in the characters' emotions. The second is the danger of actually changing from third-person to first-person in the middle of an essay. You often find yourself becoming so close to the central character that you may start off writing as 'John', and then you are somehow writing as 'I' after a few paragraphs. There is nothing more distracting for a reader and it suggests a lack of thought and preparation on the student's part. It is easy to avoid this problem if you do all your thinking beforehand.

To sum up: when using this narrative method,

1. Don't become hopelessly entangled in the central character's feelings.
2. Keep up the interest in characters and emotions as well as incidents, but
3. Still make use of your ability to 'play God': move around geographically and give insights into the thoughts of different characters.

Here are examples of both third- and first-person narrative, both from Charles Dickens:

Third-person Narrative

It was a town of red brick, or of brick that would have been red if the smoke and ashes had allowed it; but, as matters stood, it was a town of un-natural red and black like the painted face of a savage.

(from *Hard Times* by Charles Dickens)

First-person Narrative

I was brought up, from my earliest remembrance – like some of the princesses in the fairy stories, only I was not charming – by my godmother. At least I only knew her as such . . . She was handsome; and if she had ever smiled, would have been (I used to think) like an angel – but she never smiled.

(from *Bleak House* by Charles Dickens)

Once you have settled on your narrative viewpoint you are at last ready to write.

Opening Paragraph

There is no doubt that this is the most crucial part of your story. If you win your readers over in the first few lines, they will want to read on. If you lose them at this early stage, you will have to work doubly hard to win them back. So it is well worth giving the opening paragraph your best shot, and spending quite a few minutes' thought on it.

There are numerous ways of opening a piece of fiction, but this paragraph must fulfil the following functions:

1. It must catch your readers' attention at once. They should feel that they can't take their eyes off the page.
2. It must plunge them into the heart of the story.
3. It must have obvious relevance to your story-line and not just be a piece of clever writing.

You can fulfil these purposes in various ways. To mention just a few: you could shock your reader with a crisp, startling opening sentence; you could go straight into a well-written, perhaps slightly mysterious, conversation which goes to the heart of your story's meaning; you could set the scene of your story with some atmospheric description; or you could introduce one of your main characters.

You can probably think of other ways, but we'll look at these four methods for the moment, examining how some real experts tackle their opening paragraphs. We'll start with some particularly effective shock tactics:

> Hale knew they meant to murder him before he had been in Brighton three hours. With his inky fingers and his bitten nails, his manner cynical and nervous, anybody could tell he didn't belong – belong to the early summer sun, the cool Whitsun wind off the sea, the holiday crowd.

> (*Brighton Rock* by Graham Greene)

This is probably one of the most famous opening sentences in English literature. You can't help reading on! But not only does Graham Greene startle you, he also sets the scene in a condensed yet very effective way. He tells you a number of things about Hale and about where he is. He is cynical, nervous, inky-fingered, and an outsider; he is in Brighton at Whitsun, amongst a 'holiday crowd'. It is a masterpiece of compressed meaning – every word is weighted with significance.

Quite different is the leisurely opening of Alan Garner's eerie novel *The Owl Service*:

'How's the bellyache, then?'

Gwyn stuck his head round the door. Alison sat in the iron bed with brass knobs. Porcelain columns showed the Infant Bacchus and there was a lump of slate under one leg because the floor dipped.

'A bore,' said Alison. 'And I'm too hot.'

'Tough,' said Gwyn. 'I couldn't find any books, so I've brought one I had from school. I'm supposed to be reading it for Literature, but you're welcome: it looks deadly.'

'Thanks anyway,' said Alison.

'Roger's gone for a swim. You wanting company, are you?'

'Don't put yourself out for me,' said Alison.

'Right,' said Gwyn. 'Cheerio.'

He rode sideways down the bannisters on his arms to the first floor landing.

'Gwyn!'

'Yes? What's the matter? You O K?'

'Quick!'

'You want a basin? You going to throw up, are you?'

'Gwyn!'

He ran back. Alison was kneeling on the bed.

'Listen,' she said. 'Can you hear that?'

'That what?'

'That noise in the ceiling. Listen.'

The house was quiet. Mostyn Lewis-Jones was calling after the sheep on the mountain: a something was scratching in the ceiling above the bed.

'Mice,' said Gwyn.

'Too loud,' said Alison.

'Rats, then.'

'No. Listen. It's something hard.'

'They want their claws trimming.'

'It's not rats,' said Alison.

(*The Owl Service* by Alan Garner)

This method of introducing characters through dialogue is also very effective. We learn about Gwyn and Alison by listening to them, and little details tell us about their surroundings. We can tell that they are young, because Gwyn mentions school. Not only do we know that Alison is ill in bed, we also know exactly what her bed looks like (see paragraph 2). We can tell that they have quite a close relationship, but not so close that they forget to say 'thanks' (as brothers and sisters sometimes do). Somebody else is going to be introduced into the story (Roger) and we also realize from the mention of 'sheep on the mountain' that they are in the countryside. The names Mostyn Lewis-Jones and Gwyn, and the unusual lilt of Gwyn's voice ('You going to throw up, are you?' instead of '*You're* going to throw up, are you?') tell us that they are Welsh.

While he is slipping in this information, Alan Garner is also making us feel thoroughly uneasy. He presents Alison's own fear and arouses our curiosity in the phrase 'a something was scratching in the ceiling'. Again, you can't wait to read on.

Now, an opening to a frightening story, *The Fall of the House of Usher*, by Edgar Allan Poe. It is a splendid piece of scene-setting:

During the whole of a dull, dark, and soundless day in the autumn of the year, when the clouds hung oppressively low in the heavens, I had been passing alone, on horseback, through a singularly dreary tract of country; and at length found myself, as the shades of evening drew on, within view of the melancholy House of Usher.

(*The Fall of the House of Usher* by Edgar Allan Poe)

We are introduced to the central character (note the use of the first person!) and we learn that he had been travelling through the countryside on horseback. Poe creates the atmosphere of a dark and dismal autumn day through his use of adjectives, which build up through the paragraph: 'dull, dark and soundless', 'dreary', 'melancholy'. Again, every detail and every word has to tell.

Finally – something a little lighter. As some of you may already know, Jane Austen has a sure touch with opening paragraphs, and indeed with all her characters. Here she introduces us to one of her most attractive heroines:

Emma Woodhouse, handsome, clever, and rich, with a comfortable home and happy disposition, seemed to unite some of the best blessings of existence; and had lived nearly twenty-one years in the world with very little to distress or vex her.

(*Emma* by Jane Austen)

The description of Emma is exact. There is also a slight hint that something *is* about to come along and disturb this fortunate young woman. You want to read on to see if it does!

So, do spend time on your opening paragraph, but still remember that you do, after all, have to write a whole story. Keep it short and to the point and keep your readers panting for more!

Characters

However good your initial story-line may be, however compelling your opening paragraph, the story won't hold your readers' interest unless the people who take part in it are interesting and convincing. When you are reading a story or novel, you always know when you meet a character who seems to 'come to life'. You probably wonder why that is. In fact, if you looked closely at your favourite characters, you would probably find that the writers who created them were using similar techniques to make them real, which you too can learn to use.

First of all, you need to develop your own *powers of observation*. Train yourself to notice things about people and you can use some of these in your character sketches, which must be full of *significant details*. Most really successful writers use their own experience in their books and stories. They would not be successful writers if they were the sort of people who wandered around aimlessly with their eyes shut. In fact, when we don't pay much attention to what is going on under our noses, we are missing the material for a few hundred short stories.

Think of your journey to school in the morning. Have a look at some of the people around you and ask yourself some questions about them. Try to create word pictures of them in your mind. What colours are their hair and eyes? What are the shapes of their faces? Do they have any strange habits or facial peculiarities? Do they look happy or depressed? What are they wearing? Where do you think they might live? What kind of animals do they remind you of?

If you put together all you have observed, you could aim for something like this:

Timothy Gedge was a youth of fifteen, ungainly due to adolescence, a boy with a sharp-boned face and wide, thin shoulders, whose short hair was almost white. His eyes seemed hungry, giving him a predatory look; his cheeks had a hollowness about them. He was always dressed in the same clothes: pale yellow jeans and a yellow jacket with a zip, and a T-shirt that more often than not was yellow also. He lived with his mother and his sister, Rose-Ann, in a block of council-built flats called Cornerways; without distinction, he attended Dynmouth Comprehensive School. He was a boy who was given to making jokes, a habit that caused him sometimes to seem eccentric. He smiled and grinned a lot.

(*The Children of Dynmouth* by William Trevor)

The physical description is thorough and very straightforward but the filling in of Timothy's background, although sketchy, is just enough to give us quite a clear picture of the kind of life he might lead. Similarly, the short sentence, 'He smiled and grinned a lot', although it contains a very small piece of information, makes us feel rather uneasy. William Trevor also hints at what Timothy reminds him of: 'His eyes seemed hungry, giving him a predatory look.' He seems like a predator, a creature who preys on other animals. Already we have a definite idea of the kind of boy he is.

Dickens, who specializes in giving us brief but clear impressions of characters, uses a similar comparison to describe 'Gaffer' Hexam:

He was a hook-nosed man, and with that and his bright eyes and his ruffled head, bore a certain likeness to a roused bird of prey.

(*Our Mutual Friend* by Charles Dickens)

But as you can see, he draws a much closer parallel than William Trevor. This kind of careful use of comparison can be extremely effective, providing you don't overdo it. You can sometimes give a much fuller picture of someone by saying who or what they remind you of. For instance, a thin and ungainly woman with a hooked nose, eyes that stick out and brightly coloured make-up might remind you of a green and blue parrot. You need to be careful here, though, as too many comparisons can overload an essay. It is also very easy to fall into the trap of coming up with a cliché such as a woman with a fussy hairstyle reminding you of a poodle. Go for more unfamiliar, personal comparisons – similarities which have struck you at some point when you were looking at someone.

Dickens is also a master of the kind of 'impressionistic' descriptions in which he gives a few condensed details about a character, and one (perhaps unusual) feature, that might make this character stand out:

He is a mild, bald, timid man, with a shining head, and a scrubby clump of black hair sticking out at the back.

(*Our Mutual Friend* by Charles Dickens)

This is a useful technique for you to learn, as it enables you to give a clear picture in a very few words, vitally important if you are writing in timed conditions. Such descriptions can develop into 'caricature', where a certain feature, such as big ears, is blown up out of all proportion so that you think of the person as just a big nose, or, in the case of one of Dickens' caricatures, a set of shiny white teeth. It is a similar technique to that used in cartoons, and

you should probably avoid letting your character sketches turn into caricatures too frequently, unless you are a very confident writer indeed and want
to make your readers laugh.

Characters also reveal themselves through their actions and a sure way of
bringing a character to life is to give an example of how they behave. Make
use of their *gestures* and their *actions* – the way they move, the expressions on
their faces, how they eat. A single gesture can tell us as much about a
character as a paragraph of description, as the following extract demonstrates:

She laughed again, as if she said something very witty, and held my hand for a moment,
looking up into my face, promising that there was no-one in the world she so much
wanted to see. That was a way she had.

(*The Great Gatsby* by F. Scott Fitzgerald)

You can also reveal a great deal about your characters when you let them
speak. This can be a terrible stumbling block, so beware. It is all too easy to
write *very* bad dialogue. The best thing to do is to try to echo the tones of real
voices – voices you yourself have heard – in your essays. This is where you
need to be strict with yourself in pushing out of your mind half-remembered
TV programmes and films. Think to yourself: how would this character
sound if I met him or her in the street?

Have a look at this masterly dialogue between an old man and one of the
boys who had broken into his house in his absence:

'I'm terribly sorry, Mr Thomas. One of us got taken short and we thought you
wouldn't mind, and now he can't get out.'
'What do you mean, boy?'
'He's got stuck in your loo.'
'He'd no business . . . haven't I seen you before?'
'You showed me your house.'
'So I did. So I did. That doesn't give you the right to . . .'
'Do hurry, Mr Thomas. He'll suffocate.'
'Nonsense. He can't suffocate. Wait till I put my bag in.'
'I'll carry your bag.'
'Oh no you don't. I carry my own.'
'This way, Mr Thomas.'
'I can't get in the garden that way. I've got to go through the house.'
'But you can get in the garden this way, Mr Thomas. We often do.'
'You often do?' He followed the boy with a scandalized fascination.
'When? What right . . . ?'

'Do you see? The wall's low.'

'I'm not going to climb walls into my own garden. It's absurd.'

'This is how we do it. One foot here, one foot there, and over.'

The boy's face peered down, an arm shot out, and Mr Thomas found his bag taken and deposited on the other side of the wall.

(*The Destructors* by Graham Greene)

You don't need any indication about who is speaking because Greene has so carefully differentiated between the old man's rather irritable tones and the boy's self-confident, mocking voice. It is a very unnerving extract, and we never for a minute feel that there is anything forced or false about the way either of these characters is speaking, as they are reacting to each other in a realistic, convincing manner. Note, too, that Graham Greene never lets his plot grind to a halt. He is constantly moving the story on. There is no pointless dialogue: every sentence has its own importance.

You, too, should try to avoid any dialogue that is not relevant to your story in some way. Always keep things moving: make sure that every conversation advances the plot or throws new light on a character. Idle dialogue is boring and wastes valuable time.

A word, too, about *dialect*; that is, trying to record the sounds of different accents as in this sentence: ' 'E said 'e wos in the 'Ospittle but I didn't know whevver 'e wos tellin' the troof!' This may be accurate, but it, again, wastes time. You have to think about it so carefully, and it is irritating to read. Don't make things difficult for yourself!

It often helps to imagine the people you are describing in a certain *setting*, which in some way throws more light on their personalities. When you do this, you are helping your readers to 'see' your characters moving in their own surroundings. Laurie Lee brings his mother to life for us partly by creating such a very clear picture of the place with which he always associated her – the kitchen:

That kitchen, worn by our boots and lives, was scruffy, warm, and low, whose fuss of furniture seemed never the same but was shuffled around each day. A black grate crackled with coal and beech-twigs: towels toasted on the guard: the mantel was littered with fine old china, horse brasses, and freak potatoes. On the floor were strips of muddy matting, the windows were choked with plants, the walls supported stopped clocks and calendars, and smoky fungus ran over the ceilings. There were also six tables of different sizes, some armchairs gapingly stuffed, boxes, stools, and unravelling baskets, books and papers on every chair, a sofa for cats, a harmonium for coats, and a piano for dust and photographs.

(*Cider with Rosie* by Laurie Lee)

We'll come back to scene-setting later in this sub-section, and again in the section on Descriptive Essays. For the moment, remember that a description of a place is not simply decorative. It can serve, as it does in the above extract, to tell the reader more about a character's personality.

To sum up: when you are creating your characters, remember:

1. Describe *real* people, not characters from films or TV.
2. Make use of your characters' gestures and mannerisms.
3. Use comparisons sparingly.
4. Make your dialogue sound convincing, and don't fill the whole essay with conversations.
5. Use dialogue to advance the story and to develop characters.
6. Give your characters a concrete setting.

Local Colour

You won't have any room in your stories for the kind of long and thorough descriptions you might include in a descriptive essay. However, you do need to give your reader the feeling that he is finding out about real people in real places that he can see, smell – even feel.

Aim at including short descriptive sentences regularly throughout your essay so that it is easy for your readers to 'see' what is happening. The trick is to have the story playing through, almost like a film, in your mind. That way, when you change scenes it will be quite natural for you to slip in a sentence or two about the characters' surroundings, as this writer does when she describes a road at twilight, as it seems to a little girl:

It was growing dark. The street lamps were being lit. The lamp-lighter was poking his stick up into the little trap-door; the trees in the front gardens made a wavering network of shadow on the pavement; the pavement stretched before her broad and dark.

(*The Years* by Virginia Woolf)

The next extract appeals more obviously to our sense of sight and smell. It is twilight again, and this time an unhappy woman is trying to calm her nerves:

The front garden was a small square with a privet hedge. There she stood, trying to soothe herself with the scent of flowers and the fading, beautiful evening. Opposite her small gate was the stile that led uphill, under the tall hedge, between the burning glow of the cut pastures. The sky overhead throbbed and pulsed with light. The glow sank quickly off the field; the earth and the hedges smoked dusk. As it grew dark, a ruddy glare came out on the hilltop and out of the glare the diminished commotion of the fair.

(*Sons and Lovers* by D. H. Lawrence)

We can *see*, very precisely, where she is standing. We can *smell* cut grass and flowers. Looking up, we see the colour of the sky. In the distance, we can *hear* the faint sounds of the fair. It couldn't be clearer.

Remember that generalization kills a description stone dead. Look again at the extract from *The Owl Service*. When Alan Garner mentions the bed, he does not just mention any bed, but one that he can obviously see very clearly in his mind's eye. It is an 'iron bed with brass knobs' and there is 'a lump of slate under one leg because the floor dipped'. This is exactly the kind of precisely observed detail you should aim at including in *your* essays. They make your writing so much more convincing.

There is another way in which you can make use of description in your narrative essays, and that is to express a character's emotions. In such a description, we not only get a picture of the character's surroundings but also a much clearer impression of how he feels. These effects are obtained by showing how the surroundings look *to the character*. So, if he is depressed, his surroundings reflect his depression. In George Eliot's *Middlemarch*, Dorothea, the heroine, returns to her married home after her honeymoon with a rather dried-up middle-aged bore, realizing she has made a terrible mistake. Everything she sees depresses her and seems to reflect her own melancholy:

Mr and Mrs Casaubon, returning from their wedding journey, arrived at Lowick Manor in the middle of January. A light snow was falling as they descended at the door, and in the morning, when Dorothea passed from her dressing-room into the blue-green boudoir . . . she saw the long avenue of limes lifting their trunks from a white earth, and spreading white branches against the dun and motionless sky. The distant flat shrank in uniform whiteness and low-hanging uniformity of cloud. The very furniture in the room seemed to have shrunk since she saw it before; the stag in the tapestry looked more like a ghost in his ghostly blue-green world; the volumes of polite literature in the bookcase looked more like immovable imitations of books . . . The duties of her married life, contemplated as so great beforehand seemed to be shrinking with the furniture and the white vapour-walled landscape.

(*Middlemarch* by George Eliot)

Every word in this passage has been chosen to reflect a feeling of disappointment. Dorothea had high hopes of her marriage. The honeymoon has not been a success and so when she gets back everything seems less glamorous, less hopeful, than she thought. It is snowing; everything is 'white', 'dun', 'ghostly', 'blue-green' – shadowy; the clouds seem to be pressing down; the verb 'to shrink' is used three times. Reading it, we are aware of exactly how she feels – and may even start feeling the same.

So, the local colour in your narrative essays should be

1. Brief and very precise; describe a chair which you can see in your mind's eye, not just *any* chair.
2. Sensuous: appeal to your reader's senses by describing things that he can see, hear, smell, touch and taste.
3. Relevant to the story: don't just put it in because it looks good.

Pace

Before you began to write your story, you should have decided on its main incidents, its characters, and the ending you are working towards. When you are writing, you need to be conscious of the *pace* at which your story is going.

No one likes going on a car journey where the scenery is the same all the way, the car is going at a steady 50 mph, and there are no breaks or surprises. It is the same with a story. Again, think of all those easily bored readers and try to give them as much variety as possible.

You could begin with a sensational opening, then slow down and build up again at the end. Or, you could move from a leisurely opening, and create a feeling of mounting excitement rising to a climax at the end of the story. Dialogue, description and scene changes all help you to vary the pace of a story. Don't let the essay turn into what I call an 'and then' essay: 'John opened the door and then he went down the drive and then he remembered . . .' A catalogue of events with nothing to liven it up is great if you can't sleep, but you don't want the examiners to use your essay instead of a sleeping pill.

The Words You Use

Words don't just have meanings. They are also things that you listen to. If you ignore the sounds of the words you use, you are missing out on part of their function. When we read a book, a lot of the time we can't help imagining it being read aloud in our minds. That is why it is possible to pick out dialogue that doesn't work – because we read not only with our eyes, but with our ears.

So, choose words for their sounds as well as for their meanings, and this will help you to say what you want to say even more precisely. For instance, if you want to create the atmosphere of a long hot day you can use the sounds of your words to help you. 'The bees droned lazily, staggering drunkenly from flower to flower' *sounds* very different from 'The door crashed shut, he pounded down the footpath, flung open the gate and stood on the pavement, gazing about him wildly'. If you look at the verbs in the first sentence ('droned', 'staggering') and compare them with those in the second sentence, ('crashed', 'pounded', 'flung'), you realize that the mental picture we get of the action taking place is very different. One is lazy and clumsy, the other full of vigorous action and noise. If you listen to the words it becomes obvious that much of the effect actually comes from their sound, as the writer uses both their meanings and their impact when spoken aloud to convey his meaning to us.

Don't forget, too, that you need to select the words you choose for your characters especially carefully. The words they use must fit in with their ages, backgrounds and personalities. As in the extract from 'The Destructors', you should be able to tell who is speaking just by looking at what is said.

And Finally . . .

Your ending. You should have had this in your mind since the very beginning. It doesn't have to be shocking or to provide the kind of 'twist in the tale' that Roald Dahl specializes in. It just has to be satisfying. If your story is carefully worked out in the first place, the ending should not present a problem. Try not to lead your readers astray, disappointing them at the end by leaving loose ends. Think to yourself: if I was reading this story, would I believe in this, or would I feel cheated? Your ending should be both satisfying and convincing, but it need not be remarkable.

There are certain stock phrases and clichés that are guaranteed to make your teacher or examiner see red. I think they would make you see red, too, if you had to read them ten or twenty times a day. They include, 'It was all a dream', 'Will I ever know?', '. . . Or was it?' and, worst of all, a series of dots. These are the last resorts of writers who can't think of anything else to say. The ending has arrived unexpectedly thirty seconds before their time is up, and it shows. Don't fall into the trap – think of your ending *first*.

Ask Yourself Some Questions

Over the two years of your GCSE course, you should begin to develop the ability to look at your own work critically, and to see where you are going wrong. You can do this by asking yourself these questions about your writing, and answering them honestly.

1. Is the essay carefully planned? Does it have a definite shape?
2. Is the story itself convincing? Too ambitious for a short story? Clichéd? Too full of blood, guts, drugs?
3. Is the opening paragraph effective?
4. Is the point of view well chosen? Would it have been better seen from another angle?
5. Do the characters seem real? Are they described in a way which brings them easily to your mind?
6. When they speak, do they sound like real people?
7. Is there any unnecessary dialogue?
8. Is there enough local colour to give the story its own atmosphere? Is there too much description, not enough action?
9. Is the story's pace varied, or is it too slow? Do events follow one another too quickly?
10. Is the ending satisfying and convincing?

To write a story which satisfies you, and in which you know you have done your best, is a very rewarding experience. Enjoy your writing, don't be put off by failure, and keep reading, to pick up hints from other writers. You could not do better than to aim at writing like Susan Hill. Look at how much she packs into the following extract: first-rate dialogue, showing how one character is persecuting another; brief but accurate description; insight into the mind of the central character, Kingshaw; plot advancement – by the end of the extract, the story has moved on.

All the doors up here were painted brown, and after the first landing, there was no carpet. Kingshaw thought, I hate this house, I hate it, it is the very worst of all the places we have lived in. From the first moment he had looked at it, out of the car window, he had hated it. It didn't seem much for Hooper to be so proud of.

He walked along a little, dark passage-way, and turned into the corridor. Then he saw Hooper. He was sitting on the floor, with his back against the door of the room and his legs stretched out. Kingshaw stopped dead.

'Going somewhere?'

'Get lost, Hooper.'

'Where's the key? Look, this isn't your house, you know, who do you think you are, going around locking doors.'

'Stuff it!'

'You can't come in here any more unless I say so.'

Kingshaw put down the small box he was carrying, wearily. Hooper was very childish.

'You needn't think I'm going away, either. I can stay here all day. All night as well, if I like. I can stay here for ever. This is my house.'

'Why don't you grow up?'

'I want to know what's in here.'

'Nothing.'

'That means something. You'd better tell me.'

'Shut up.'

'I want to know what you keep coming up here for. You needn't think I don't know where you go to. I've known for weeks, all the time, I've known.'

Kingshaw was silent. He stood some way back from Hooper, his face in the shadows. There was the sound of rain on the roof. He might as well let Hooper in. He'd get in, anyway, fight, or else just stick it out for hours on end. He had no good opinion of his own chances, against Hooper. Or against anyone. He was not cowardly. Just realistic, hopeless. He did not give in to people, he only went, from the beginning, with the assurance that he would be beaten. It meant that there was no surprise, and no disappointment, about anything.

So he might as well let Hooper into the room now, and get it over with. If he was going to find out, he might as well find out because Kingshaw chose to let him. It kept the initiative in his hands, somehow, and he cared about that. Hooper always won.

Kingshaw reached slowly into the back pocket of his jeans, and fetched out the key.

(*I'm the King of the Castle* by Susan Hill)

DESCRIPTIVE ESSAYS

You describe both places and people in your stories, to make them more interesting and realistic. You can also choose to write an essay where the main interest is in the creation of the atmosphere of a particular place.

They differ from narrative and autobiographical essays in that they do not really require any dialogue or even a story-line. What they do demand from you are razor-sharp powers of observation and the ability to record precisely what you have experienced through your own senses. If these sound very much like the talents you might need to be a good foreign correspondent for a newspaper or a successful travel writer, you are quite right. You don't need great imaginative powers to master these writing skills, but a heightened sense of awareness and a greater than usual attention to detail.

The very first thing to get clear in your mind before you even attempt to describe a place, is the exact effect you wish to create, whether it is to be positive or negative. For instance, you could describe the same place as either 'My Favourite Place' or 'The Place I Hate Most'. For each passage, you would need to select completely different details to make your readers feel that this is the kind of place they would like to see, or to put them off it.

To help you to sort out the kind of details you might need, think of a town or city you know well. First, make a list of all the things you like about the place, such as a park with fountains or a particular line of shops. Then, list all the things you dislike about it, such as over-full litter bins, a building site, or traffic congestion. A glance over your two lists will demonstrate easily how you could build up a very full description by focusing in on certain areas and rearranging individual details. Don't be vague. Select small details to activate a scene, like a close-up on TV, then pan out with your camera to create a more impressionistic but still accurate picture. Always keep your eye on how you want your reader to feel about this place.

Look at Émile Zola's description of a Paris back street. Pick out the original, precisely observed details he uses, and think of the kind of impression he was aiming at:

At the end of the rue Guenugaud, as you come up from the river, you find the Passage du Pont-Neuf, a sort of narrow, dark corridor connecting rue Mazarine and rue de Seine. This passage is thirty yards long and two in width at the most; it is paved with yellowish flagstones, worn and loose, which always exude a damp, pungent smell, and it is covered with a flat, glazed roofing black with grime.

On fine summer days, when the streets are baking in the oppressive heat, a whitish light does fall through the dingy glass roofing and hang dismally about this arcade, but on nasty winter ones, on foggy mornings, the panes send down nothing but gloom on to the greasy pavement below, and dirty, evil gloom at that.

(*Thérèse Raquin* by Émile Zola)

Zola is using the close-up camera technique, here. Virginia Woolf, in this next extract, lets her camera rove all over the deserted house she is describing, picking out the details she needs to create an atmosphere of desolation, melancholy and peace:

The house was left; the house was deserted. It was left like a shell on a sandhill to fill with dry salt grains now that life had left it. The long night seemed to have set in . . . The saucepan had rusted and the mat decayed. Toads had nosed their way in. Idly, aimlessly, the swaying shawl swung to and fro. A thistle thrust itself between the tiles in the larder. The swallows nested in the drawing-room; the floor was strewn with straw; the plaster fell in shovelfuls; rafters were laid bare; rats carried off this and that to gnaw behind the wainscots. Tortoise-shell butterflies burst from the chrysalis and pattered their life out on the windowpanes.

(*To the Lighthouse* by Virginia Woolf)

Picture Essays

Very observant, imaginative writers can produce excellent essays based on pictures. It is also very easy to degenerate into either a very loose story, vaguely connected with one detail in your picture, or merely to record, verbally, what is actually in the picture. The GCSE examiners constantly stress the need to use your powers of analysis and imagination to move out from and elaborate on the material you are given as 'stimulus' – in this case, the picture itself. Always bear in mind the idea that the picture is a *basis* for your writing, and you must neither move too far away from it in your essay, nor become too bogged down in one idea.

When you are given a picture for a coursework assignment or in the examination itself, if you are sitting one, study it very carefully, and with a completely open mind, thinking of the various possibilities it suggests. You could start by asking questions about it. Who is the person in the right-hand corner, and what is he doing? What time of day is it? What are the characters looking at? Why does the central character look sad? You might find that this process sparks off some ideas; then there are a number of different angles you could take on the one idea that interests you most. You could *become* one of the figures in a picture or photograph and write about what you think is happening from that person's point of view, exploring his or her feelings. You could focus on one particular aspect of the picture and develop a story out of it, though never moving too far away from your original inspiration. You could pick out one person in the picture and write a story around him or her. Why are they there? Where do they live? The questions are endless. Or, you might give a panoramic view of the scene from an observer's point of view, developing it and making sure that it doesn't turn into a rather dull catalogue of what you see. If it is a picture of a landscape you could explore what gives that landscape its peculiar quality, perhaps from the perspective of a person who lives there.

Once you have decided what to do with the picture your greatest enemy is irrelevance. It is all too easy to immerse yourself in your story and its characters, losing sight of its original basis altogether. So *keep looking at the picture!* Just continue to tell yourself that everything you say must seem probable and convincing when you look back at your original source. Don't let yourself wander off, make up too many characters or interpret the scene in an unlikely way, perhaps writing about an outdoor occasion when the scene represented is quite clearly indoors.

When you are writing, bear in mind your guidelines for the other types of essay discussed so far and you should find this kind of essay very satisfying.

To sum up. When writing descriptive or picture essays, remember:

1. Don't generalize.
2. Include small, significant details.
3. Appeal to the senses.
4. Keep thinking about the effect you want to create.

AUTOBIOGRAPHICAL ESSAYS

It must have become obvious from the previous two sections that nearly everything you write in the descriptive or narrative form needs to have some basis in your own experience if it is to be convincing. In this section we'll consider how to make the best of those essays which are very clearly intended to be drawn more closely from your own life. A few titles in this vein – and some of them must be depressingly familiar – are 'A Day to Remember', 'My First Day at School', 'The Most Important Day of my Life'. The GCSE examiners specifically require you to 'articulate experience and express what is felt and what is imagined', and this kind of essay gives you the ideal opportunity to do just that.

What you are being required to do, for any of these titles, is imaginatively to rework an experience which meant a great deal *to you*, and which you can remember in some detail. Now, just because something which happens is very important to you does not necessarily mean it has to be disturbing or sensational or even very special. You need to convey the feelings you had so vividly that the reader is able to share them with you and to sympathize with and understand the importance of the incident. One of the best essays I have ever read was about a lost teddy bear: the anguish of the child was so accurately portrayed that you were absolutely desperate, by the end of the essay, for her to rediscover this unfortunate toy.

If, for instance, you were given the title 'A Day to Remember', the first thing you might do is jot down ideas at random using the method illustrated on p. 11. From these ideas, you should pick out *two* incidents, which you can remember very well but which may not have happened on the same day, and concentrate on bringing those to life. You may be lucky: you may just have had a particularly awful or exciting day, the fresh memories of which you will be able to use with great ease. It will help you considerably if you have accurate sensory recollections of the scenes and people involved, so that you are re-creating characters and places rather than trying to invent them.

Before you start, check that you have *sufficient material* for a 400+ word essay. The incidents on which you wish to concentrate must be sufficiently significant to carry the reader's interest so you must be confident that you can breathe real vitality into them. You should also make sure that you don't go to the other extreme of *not* limiting yourself and waffling on without any apparent aim. Although narrative as such is not important – after all, the plot involved is that of your own life – you must plan the essay as scrupulously as if it were a story, excluding anything which is not strictly relevant and concentrating on building up the significance of your one or two main events. Don't be tempted to reminisce, to spill out various memories with no particular structure: it might all be very honest and accurate, but it certainly won't be very interesting.

You also need to sort out your 'point of view', as with a narrative essay. Obviously, you will be writing as 'I' but there are several possible pitfalls here. The first is that of giving in to the temptation of writing as somebody else. Be yourself – that way, you won't fall into the fatal trap of sounding insincere. The second pitfall is that of trying to write from the point of view of yourself as you were at the time about which you are writing. To be specific: if you are writing about your first day at school, you must *never* try to imitate the vocabulary of a five-year-old. You are looking back on certain events and seeing them from the point of view of a fifteen- or sixteen-year-old who can still see how important these incidents were but who is now a detached observer.

For instance, the girl writing about the lost teddy bear tried to express both the desolation of the three-year-old child *and* the detached amusement and sympathy of herself at fifteen. Similarly, Laurie Lee in the opening paragraph of *Cider with Rosie* conveys both the marvellous excitement of being a child in a new, magic world, and also gives us a sense that the older Laurie is perhaps looking back as a wiser, more experienced character, and rather longing for the innocence of childhood:

I was set down from the carrier's cart at the age of three; and there with a sense of bewilderment and terror my life in the village began.

The June grass amongst which I stood, was taller than I was and I wept. I had never been so close to grass before. It towered above me and all around me, each blade tattooed with tiger-skins of sunlight. It was knife-edged, dark, and a wicked green, thick as a forest and alive with grasshoppers that chirped and chattered and leapt through the air like monkeys.

(*Cider with Rosie* by Laurie Lee)

This extract should also illustrate the importance of a totally gripping opening paragraph, as in a narrative essay. You must seize your reader's attention and put him, immediately, in your world. As you are writing, remember that all the points discussed in connection with the creation of characters and places apply here, but also remember that everything must be seen from your own personal point of view and you must be absolutely sure of the effect you wish to create. For instance, Laurie Lee, again, recollecting his wanderings in Spain in *As I Walked out one Midsummer Morning* recalls the magic of Madrid:

By now it was noon, with almost everyone under cover, in the bars and moistly shaded cafés, at this hour when Madrid properly came into its own . . . Most other capitals, in such heat, would still have been an inferno of duty, full of damp shopgirls and exhausted clerks. But not here, for Madrid knew when to say No, and draw its shutters against the sun.

. . . Madrid at that time was a city of a thousand exquisite taverns – water-cooled, barrel-lined and cavernously spacious, cheap and affectionately run, in whose traditional shade the men at least, spent a half of their waking time.

Stepping in from the torrid street, you met a band of cool air like fruit-peel pressed to your brow, and entered a cloistered grotto laden with the tang of shellfish, wet tiles and wine-soaked wood. There was no waiting, no crowding; the place was yours; pot-boys took your orders with ringing cries; and men stood at their ease holding goblets of sherry with plenty of time to drink them, while piled round the counters – succulently arranged in dishes or enthroned on great blocks of ice – lay banquets of sea-food: craggy oysters, crabs, calamares heaped in golden rings, fresh lobsters twitching on beds of palm-leaves, bowls of mussels and feathery shrimps. Also on offer would be the little sizzling saucers of kidney or roasted sparrow, snails, fried squid, hot prawns in garlic, stewed pork or belly of lamb.

Note that he is not talking about one particular tavern, but is describing the most attractive features of all of them, merging them together in a general picture. All his vocabulary is chosen to suggest the contrast between the blistering heat of the sun and the cool atmosphere inside the taverns: 'torrid', 'a band of cool air', 'cloistered grotto', and 'blocks of ice'. A number of words also suggest that there is something magical about these taverns: 'grotto', 'goblets', 'banquets', 'golden rings'. He also makes a few very suggestive comparisons such as 'a band of cool air like fruit-peel pressed to your brow', which appeal directly to our senses. We can see, hear, even taste, Madrid. Probably in real life these taverns may have been nothing like as glamorous as he describes them but this is the impression of them which he has treasured, and which he wants us to share.

In a very different passage, Richard Church recalls how everything in Battersea when he was a child reminded him of a seaside town, and all the details he gives us are chosen to re-create this impression:

The Battersea that I explored was not so red in tooth and claw as I have suggested. Generally, it was a slumbrous suburb, largely peopled with artisan folk, clerks and minor Civil Servants such as my father, whose surface uniformity was deceptive.

The little streets had a character that made me think of sailors rather than industrial workers. This may have been caused by the tidal waters of the Thames that ebbed and flowed round the parish, giving it a strand of mud enlivened with washed pebbles, and salt-breasted gulls that screamed as though a herring-fleet were coming in.

The streets, too, aided the illusion, for most of the householders maintained the practice of lime-washing their yards front and back, and even the lower courses of the house-walls, to preserve the health of their copious livestock: rabbits, poultry, pigeons, and even goats. The effect of this was to give the impression of sailors ashore; of holystone and white-scrubbed decks, of painted masts, of furled sails and gleaming port-holes.

(*Over the Bridge* by Richard Church)

Even if you are a very nervous writer, try to have confidence in your ability at least to write this kind of essay. Your own thoughts and feelings, if properly expressed and well organized, will always be interesting, and will have that unmistakable ring of authenticity.

FACTUAL OR PRACTICAL WRITING

The GCSE examiners are very concerned that you have your audience in mind when you are writing and that you are able to write for a very wide variety of different purposes, adapting your style accordingly. They require you to 'order and present factual information, such as an account of an event or process, a report of a visit or interview or a piece of research'.

All the possible written assignments suggested so far allow for self-expression – some more than others, of course – but as yet you have not had to write essays where the emphasis is on facts. This is what practical writing, or factual writing as it is sometimes called, is all about. Here, you are concerned with conveying the required information in as clear, precise and simple a way as possible.

Explanations and Instructions

The most frequently used type of factual writing is the explanation, usually of a process, such as mending a puncture or grooming a horse. You will certainly need to write such an explanation at some stage in your GCSE course, so the skills must be mastered.

It is quite an art to give instructions, even for a simple process, without leaving out important details. First of all, the best way of ensuring that your instructions are logical, is to go through the process yourself, noting down every detail of your progress. You will find that, sometimes, you might tend to do things out of sequence, so when you have your list of actions you should rearrange them into the order which, on reflection, seems to you would save the most time and effort. Make your vocabulary as simple as possible. If you need to use a technical or unfamiliar term, make sure that you explain it to your readers the first time you use it. Trim the instructions down to be as brief as possible (you may find you need several drafts to reach the required brevity) and remember – leave nothing to chance. You cannot afford to leave out a single detail in explanations so your safest bet is to assume that your readers know nothing about what to do and need to be taken through the different stages slowly and clearly. The best way of testing the success of your explanations is to read them out to a younger brother or sister: if they understand them, you are all right!

Here is an accurate example for you to study.

INSTRUCTIONS FOR DEFROSTING THE FREEZER

Freezers require little day-to-day maintenance but must be defrosted occasionally. Defrost chest freezers about once or twice a year, uprights 2 or 3 times.

1. Switch off the electricity.
2. Remove all the frozen food and wrap in newspaper, blanket, insulated container or even an old sleeping bag to keep cold. Store temporarily in a cool place.
3. Leave the door or lid of the freezer open and allow to defrost.
4. The process can be speeded up by placing bowls of hot water inside the cabinet and by helping to loosen the melting ice with a wooden or plastic spatula (never a metal object as this may damage the lining of the cabinet). Old towels placed at the base of the cabinet can help to mop up the water.
5. When all the ice is melted, wipe over the inside of the cabinet with a solution of bicarbonate of soda and hot water, not detergent.
6. Dry out thoroughly.
7. Switch the freezer on, and replace the food immediately.

                              (*Collins' Practical Dictionary of Household Hints*)

Factual Description

This is the other type of factual writing we'll consider in this chapter. Again, the ability to write a concise, informative and thorough description of an area, building, company or even a person is a valuable skill and one that you will find very useful indeed, whatever career you pursue. Such a description differs from the kind of descriptive writing we have discussed earlier in that you must, of course, exclude your own feelings and responses from the piece. You are aiming, as in your explanations, at giving a clear and accurate account of something about which your audience knows nothing at all and you have a duty to them to give as truthful an impression as possible.

You should always narrow your field in such a description, and write for a very clearly defined purpose. The example below is taken from the *Guide to Britain's Nature Reserves* and illustrates how a writer can focus on a particular aspect such as wildlife for a description, excluding everything irrelevant to that purpose. If this was your description, of course, you should explain such rare technical terms as 'edge habitat', 'dabblers', and 'waders', in notes at the bottom of the description.

Talybont Reservoir
50 098190: 146ha; BNT reserve
Flooded valley reservoir
No access to the reservoir area
Autumn, winter, spring.

The reservoir is a long, narrow body of water in the steep, forested valley. Generally deep, it is ideal for diving birds, and the southern end shallows into meadowland suitable for dabblers and waders. The shores are variable, sometimes gently sloping, sometimes with shallow muddy cliffs, so the range of 'edge' habitat is considerable.

Mallard, teal and widgeon are the commonest of the dabbling ducks seen here and may be joined at the water's edge by occasional waders such as curlew, redshank, common and green sandpiper and greenshank. The waders are wonderfully adapted to their environment. Their long legs hold them above the icy waters while their long beaks probe down deep into the mud. Of course, this similarity might lead to too many species feeding on the same prey, but a range of different styles of beak ensures that each species takes a different type of food, reducing competition to a minimum.

Three of the largest birds seen at the reservoir are the swans, resident mute swan and the two winter visitors, Bewick's and whooper swan, which fly in from Russia and Northern Europe.

(*The Macmillan Guide to Britain's Nature Reserves*)

PERSUASIVE WRITING AND JOURNALISM AND DISCUSSION/ARGUMENTATIVE ESSAYS

As well as requiring you to 'articulate experience', the GCSE examiners also require an ability to 'understand, order and present facts, ideas and opinions'. In this section we'll look at the area where facts, opinions and personal feelings overlap.

In such a piece of writing, you may need to discuss the pros and cons of a particular issue, argue a case (putting your point of view forward strongly) or explore the implications of a moral issue. The title will indicate precisely what kind of essay is involved, for instance 'Are Experiments on Animals Necessary? Support your arguments with examples', 'Should Religious Education be Compulsory in Schools?' 'Is Sport a Worthwhile Activity?' – and so on.

The skills you will need to write this very challenging kind of essay are those which you will constantly find yourself using throughout your life. We are frequently in situations where we need to explain, put our point of view, convince someone and generally marshal our thoughts into some coherent order. To present a point of view or series of ideas in such a way that you can persuade and influence your readers you will need to have a logical mind, clarity, organization and general 'coolness'. You will need to be a person who can put forward a reasonable and well-argued point of view without losing your head.

First of all, it is essential that you have enough information on your topic, whether you are writing in an examination or for coursework. The subject must be something that interests you, and you need to have facts and examples at your fingertips.

This kind of essay is, in fact, an ideal coursework assignment as you have time to select your subject (perhaps choosing, with your teacher, an issue about which you feel very strongly) and to research it fully. It is very difficult to produce a well-argued and well-supported discussion essay under examination conditions unless you have thought about it beforehand. However, if you have had time to track down recent information and examples which you can use in your argument, you will be able to produce a very coherent piece of writing.

Before you even put pen to paper, you need to sort out your point of view, and to know precisely where you stand on your chosen topic. Then you can organize your material accordingly. The *structure* of the essay should be as simple as possible, demonstrating a clear line of argument. Each paragraph should treat one aspect of the subject.

Often, when you make your preliminary notes for the essay, a structure will suggest itself. For instance, in an essay which asks you to 'Give the case for and against animal experimentation' you could develop first the case for experimentation, looking at each point separately, turning in the middle of the essay

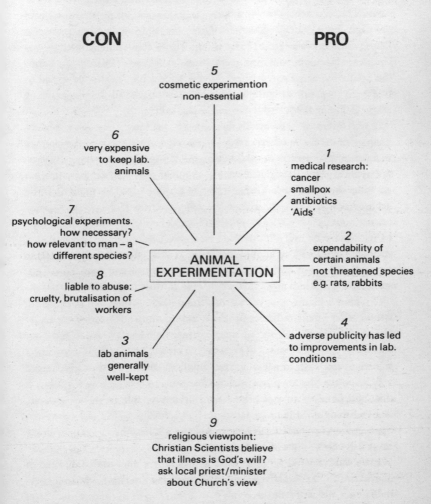

CON

PRO

5
cosmetic experimention
non-essential

6
very expensive
to keep lab.
animals

1
medical research:
cancer
smallpox
antibiotics
'Aids'

7
psychological experiments.
how necessary?
how relevant to man – a
different species?

8
liable to abuse:
cruelty, brutalisation of
workers

ANIMAL
EXPERIMENTATION

2
expendability of
certain animals
not threatened species
e.g. rats, rabbits

4
adverse publicity has led
to improvements in lab.
conditions

3
lab animals
generally
well-kept

9
religious viewpoint:
Christian Scientists believe
that illness is God's will?
ask local priest/minister
about Church's view

to the case against, keeping a definite balance, then coming to your own views at the end, so that they seem to arise out of the examples you have given.

The figure on p. 41 illustrates one possible method of planning such an essay. The arguments 'for' have been jotted down on the right-hand side of the page, the arguments against on the left. Organizing the page in this way helps you to organize your thoughts, too. If you studied these jottings, you would be able to work out a logical progression of ideas. The numbers beside the points represent a suggested order for the ideas. Each idea would be treated in a separate paragraph. You would end up with an eleven-paragraph essay, including the introduction and conclusion.

The *introduction* could briefly mention the area which the essay will cover. Each point should be stated simply and clearly and should be well supported with examples, references, and quotations if possible. Remember that you are trying to persuade and influence your audience – you want them to agree with you, so you will need to appeal both to reason and to the emotions. If you get hysterical, or out of control, no one will be convinced. Ideally, you should present your facts in such a way that they speak for themselves. There should be no need to be over-emotional. The *concluding paragraph* should suggest your own position. You should leave your reader with a definite thought to take away, perhaps with a memorable quotation or example. Avoid just summarizing the ideas you have already put forward in the essay.

Your *tone* – that is, *how* you say something – is important too. Your style of writing will be quite different from that in your more imaginative, expansive essays. You will need to be more formal and less personal and your vocabulary should be more businesslike. You will find yourself using fewer adjectives and fewer words which are 'emotive' – that is, emotionally charged words such as 'the poor unfortunate little bunnies'(!). It is also very easy, in this kind of essay, to lapse into clumsy phrases such as 'in my opinion', 'another thing is', 'due to the fact that', or 'in conclusion I would like to say'. Such phrases can become very monotonous; it is best just to get on with the essay without the useless linking phrases.

Let's have a look, now, at what a real expert does with the topic of 'Christmas'. George Orwell wrote the following article on seasonal over-indulgence just after the Second World War, in 1946, during the era of rationing, but it still sounds as fresh as ever. As you read it through, try to be alert to all the devices he uses to persuade you over to his point of view:

As I Please

An advertisement in my Sunday paper sets forth in the form of a picture the four things that are needed for a successful Christmas. At the top of the picture is a roast turkey; below that, a Christmas pudding; below that, a dish of mince pies; and below that, a tin of ——'s Liver Salt.

Starts with personal experience

It is a simple recipe for happiness. First the meal, then the antidote, then another meal. The ancient Romans were the great masters of this technique. However, having just looked up the word *vomitorium* in the Latin dictionary, I find that after all it does *not* mean a place where you went to be sick after dinner. So perhaps this was not a normal feature of every Roman home, as is commonly believed.

Summary of what Xmas has come to mean

Implied in the above-mentioned advertisement is the notion that a good meal means a meal at which you overeat yourself. In principle I agree. I only add in passing that when we gorge ourselves this Christmas, if we do get the chance to gorge ourselves, it is worth giving a thought to the thousand million human beings, or thereabouts, who will be doing no such thing. For in the long run our Christmas dinners would be safer if we could make sure that everyone else had a Christmas dinner as well. But I will come back to that presently.

Topic sentence

The only reasonable motive for not overeating at Christmas would be that somebody else needs the food more than you do. A deliberately austere Christmas would be an absurdity. The whole point of Christmas is that it is a debauch – as it was probably long before the birth of Christ was arbitrarily fixed at that date. Children know this very well. From their point of view Christmas is not a day of temperate enjoyment, but of fierce pleasures which they are quite willing to pay for with a certain amount of pain. The awakening at about 4 am to inspect your stocking; the quarrels over toys all through the morning, and the exciting whiffs of mincemeat and sage-and-onions escaping from the kitchen door; the battle with enormous platefuls of turkey, and the pulling of the wishbone; the darkening of the windows and the entry of the flaming plum pudding; the

This sentence links the two paragraphs

Topic sentence – slightly satirical tone

Examples

1

2

3

4'

hurry to make sure that everyone has a piece on his plate while the brandy is still alight; the momentary panic when it is rumoured that Baby has swallowed the threepenny bit; the stupor all through the afternoon; the Christmas cake with almond icing an inch thick; the peevishness next morning and the castor oil on December 27th – it is an up-and-down business, by no means all pleasant, but well worth while for the sake of its more dramatic moments.

He gives a different viewpoint: that of minority groups

Teetotallers and vegetarians are always scandalised by this attitude. As they see it, the only rational objective is to avoid pain and to stay alive as long as possible. If you refrain from drinking alcohol, or eating meat, or whatever it is, you may expect to live an extra five years, while if you overeat or overdrink you will pay for it in acute physical pain on the following day. Surely it follows that all excesses, even a once-a-year outbreak such as Christmas, should be avoided as a matter of course?   5

Actually it doesn't follow at all. One may decide, with full knowledge of what one is doing, that an occasional good time is worth the damage it inflicts on one's liver. For health

Topic sentence giving benefits of Xmas indulgence

is not the only thing that matters: friendship, hospitality, and the heightened spirits and change of outlook that one gets by eating and drinking in good company are also valuable. I doubt whether, on balance, even outright drunkenness does harm, provided it is infrequent – twice a year, say. The whole experience, including the repentance afterwards, makes a sort of break in one's mental routine, comparable to a weekend in a foreign country, which is probably beneficial.   6

In all ages men have realised this. There is a wide consensus of opinion, stretching back to the days before the alphabet, that whereas habitual soaking is bad, conviviality is good, even if one does sometimes feel sorry for it next morning. How enormous is the literature of eating and drinking, especially drinking, and how little that is worth while has been said on the other side! Offhand I can't

Examples from history supporting the view that the occasional celebration is good for you. This paragraph concentrates on the pleasures of drink . . .

remember a single poem in praise of water, i.e. water regarded as a drink. It is hard to imagine what one could say about it. It quenches thirst: that is the end of the story. As for poems in praise of wine, on the other hand, even the surviving ones would fill a shelf of books. The poets started turning them out on the very day when the fermentation of   7 the grape was first discovered. Whisky, brandy and other distilled liquors have been less eloquently praised, partly because they came later in time. But beer has had quite a good press, starting well back in the Middle Ages, long before anyone had learned to put hops in it. Curiously enough, I can't remember a poem in praise of stout, not even draught stout, which is better than the bottled variety, in my opinion. There is an extremely disgusting description in *Ulysses* of the stout-vats in Dublin. But there is a sort of back-handed tribute to stout in the fact that this description, though widely known, has not done much towards putting the Irish off their favourite drink.

The literature of eating is also large, though mostly in prose. But in all the writers who have enjoyed describing food, from Rabelais to Dickens and from Petronius to Mrs Beeton, I cannot remember a single passage which puts dietetic considerations first. Always food is felt to be an end in itself. No one has written memorable prose about vitamins, or the dangers of an excess of proteins, or the importance of masticating everything thirty-two times. All in all, there seems to be a heavy weight of testimony on the side of overeating and overdrinking, provided always that they take place on recognised occasions and not too frequently.

the next on the pleasures of food

8

But ought we to overeat and overdrink this Christmas? We ought not to, nor will most of us get the opportunity. I am writing in praise of Christmas, but in praise of Christmas 1947, or perhaps 1948. The world as a whole is not exactly in a condition for festivities this year. Between the Rhine and the Pacific there cannot be very many people who are in need of ——'s Liver Salt. In India there are, and always have been, about 100 million people who only get one square meal a day. In China, conditions are no doubt much the same. In Germany, Austria, Greece and elsewhere, scores of millions of people are existing on a diet which keeps breath in the body but leaves no strength for work. All over the war-wrecked areas from Brussels to Stalingrad, other uncounted millions are living in the cellars of bombed houses, in hide-outs in the forests, or in squalid huts behind barbed wire. It is not so pleasant to read almost simultaneously that a large proportion of our Christmas turkeys

He focuses on the present Christmas, in the aftermath of war

9

will come from Hungary, and that the Hungarian writers and journalists – presumably not the worst-paid section of the community – are in such desperate straits that they would be glad to receive presents of saccharine and cast-off clothing from English sympathisers. In such circumstances we could hardly have a 'proper' Christmas, even if the materials for it existed.

But we will have one sooner or later, in 1947, or 1948, or maybe even in 1949. And when we do, may there be no gloomy voices of vegetarians or teetotallers to lecture us about the things that we are doing to the linings of our stomachs. <u>One celebrates a feast for its own sake, and not for any supposed benefit to the lining of one's stomach.</u> Meanwhile Christmas is here, or nearly. Santa Claus is rounding up his reindeer, the postman staggers from door to door beneath his bulging sack of Christmas cards, the black markets are humming, and Britain has imported over 7,000 crates of mistletoe from France. So I wish everyone an old-fashioned Christmas in 1947, and meanwhile, half a turkey, three tangerines, and a bottle of whisky at not more than double the legal price.

He leaves us with his own view – expressed in a final topic sentence

10

Tribune, 20 December 1946

This very successful, thought-provoking article can be summarized as follows.

1. Orwell notices an advertisement for liver salts to cure Christmas indigestion.
2. He then reflects that even the Romans seemed to have been aware of the need to counteract overeating.
3. However, we should remember those who are hungry when we overeat at Christmas.
4. The whole point of Christmas is 'having a good time' – and he uses our common experience to support this idea.
5. He gives the view of teetotallers and vegetarians, for whom the traditional Christmas celebration is unpleasant.
6. The real point of Christmas is to enjoy the pleasures of good company and a break in routine.
7. He turns to the pleasures of drink, in literature –
8. – and the pleasures of food, supporting his argument.

9. He again appeals to his readers to think of those who are not able to enjoy themselves at Christmas.
10. He ends by wishing them a merry Christmas and stressing again the need to celebrate occasionally.

As you can see, the structure is neat and well balanced. Orwell is defending the celebration of Christmas for very humane reasons – it brings us together as a community, provides a break in routine, allows us to indulge. However, he does not ignore the very powerful arguments *against* the celebration of Christmas while so many people are suffering. He argues for thoughtfulness and consideration, but not for an extremist abandonment of the feast altogether. Examples from literature support his views and he strengthens his own main point – which he makes in paragraphs 4, 6, 7 and 10, keeping it to the forefront of our minds – by giving careful consideration to the opposition.

Magazine or Newspaper Articles

It might be well worth considering incorporating an article demonstrating journalistic skills into your coursework folder, if you have been researching a particular topic such as animal experimentation. If you chose to find out about such a subject you might well find that you become very involved in the ideas it generated and rather than writing a discussion essay you might like to present your ideas in a more flexible way. You could then imagine yourself submitting an article to a newspaper.

The same rules for structuring the piece apply as for discussion or argumentative essays but with one big difference: you can take a more personal approach, so you are able to express your feelings much more clearly and strongly. You should choose a fairly eyecatching title and arrange your arguments to make a particular point. It is still sensible not to get carried away but your tone can certainly be less formal, and you can make a more direct appeal to your readers. The best way to tone up for writing such a piece is to get used to reading these newspapers regularly, especially the features pages where there are often articles by people like yourself who just feel strongly about a subject, like the following young woman:

SIXTH FORMERS
LEARN LESSON
ABOUT AIDS

THERE was a rumour at school that someone was coming to give us a lecture on Aids. A great idea, I thought, maybe it would end all the misconceptions most people at school seem to have, particularly that Aids only affects homosexuals. I was keen to go, but surprised to discover myself in a minority. Loads of people didn't seem interested. They knew everything there was to know about Aids, they said, so why bother?

A couple of weeks later, Dr Anthony Pinching, senior lecturer at St Mary's Hospital, Paddington, London, and head of the Aids ward, arrived to give a lecture to the upper school.

At 17, I live at home and attend a girls' private day school. It has, as far as I can judge, the best adjusted mixture of academic push and open attitudes to politics and life of any similar London schools. But sometimes I get the feeling that life is made to look easier than it is, and that those in control are trying to close our eyes to what is going on in the world outside.

'By the end of his talk, the doctor had brought a rare silence over our school hall'

I've never understood why we don't have proper sex education within the school, as it is a subject that will affect my generation more than most, the extreme ignorance I have encountered among my peers may well end up being lethal.

I have studied the media coverage of Aids, but it is difficult to know what to take seriously when people get so hysterical when discussing it, sensationalising the effects, placing great importance on moral issues rather than emphasising the real and immediate threat.

Dr Pinching was given a mixed reception. He seemed rather nervous and I'm not surprised with all those girls ready to hang on to his every word. From the way he talked, I could tell he wasn't quite sure how to give a complete picture of Aids, its origins, the virus itself, its spread and prevention.

First he defined the high risk groups. Then he gave us an explanation of the African origins of the disease and outlined the problems of controlling such an epidemic in under-developed countries. Next he tackled the actual construction of the virus, drawing diagrams and using slides, describing how it attacked the body's immune system and why, once infected, there is only a slight chance of recovery.

Having said all this comprehensibly, he then tackled the hardest part, spread and control. I was impressed by the way he dealt with this; we had all expected him to emphasise the moral issues, conforming to normal social policy, but he stuck to the point and was very direct. The unembarrassed way in which he tackled sex and promiscuity I think surprised most of his now-spellbound audience.

● A 17-year-old girl says younger children should be told the truth

---

The only point I felt Dr Pinching dealt with in an unrealistic manner was that of drug abuse and related anti-social behaviour. He gave the impression that any drug taken in any quantity could lead to infection with the Aids virus, frightening many who have recently been experimenting with the odd joint. To prevent any panic I think he should have made a clearer distinction between that and jacking up with unhygienic needles filled with smack.

By the end of his talk, Dr Pinching had brought a rare silence over our school hall, which had been initially filled with quiet murmuring and an interested hum. He then invited questions, and although most were about serious matters like rape, accidental blood loss and government legislation, a few raised giggles from the younger contingent and exposed the general ignorance that still exists among them.

I think all who attended the lecture had been interested, owing to Dr Pinching's efforts. The event had been a general success from which most of us had learned at least one or two things. But I couldn't help wondering what the excluded lower school were thinking about Aids. They are on the verge of discovering 'sex and drugs and rock 'n' roll', so why weren't they included? Surely this important issue should be documented more widely and not be denied to intelligent 14-year-old girls.

The general feeling now is that the school is waking up to its responsibilities as far as sex is concerned, maybe sex education over and above the basic biological facts of the science syllabus should be made a fixture in the school curriculum to help counter the general unawareness of the Aids problem, not to mention birth control and so on.

The talk did a lot to clarify some very confusing issues that affect us. Personally, it has prompted serious thought about the 1980s' so-called sophisticated sexual equality and frequent promiscuity. I know I will think carefully about embarking on future relationships, but I worry whether the people I face every day will take Aids into consideration as well.

Pola Wickham
(aged 17)

Sometimes it can be extremely rewarding to play the observant reporter and find out about an area and its residents, writing up your findings in an article. If you are lucky enough to live in or near a town or district which you know well and which interests you, GCSE provides a marvellous opportunity for you to do something fascinating *and* to get marks for it. You could look, briefly, at the history of the area, try to bring out something of its character in the present day, interview residents (perhaps your friends' parents) about their memories and find out some details from the local council about any plans to alter the face of the area (such as large-scale building in the future). Once you have amassed your research, including a map of the area and perhaps a few photographs, you can easily make it into a most interesting article.

Reviews

A further way in which you can demonstrate your journalistic skills is through a book, film or theatre review. It must be said, however, that there is not really much point in presenting a review of popular commercial films and books as you can rest assured that the comments you can make on such works, enjoyable though they may be, will be rather limited. You should choose to review works which do have some artistic merit and about which you can be sure that you will be able to think of plenty to say. The safest thing to do is to check with your teacher before you waste your time. Ideally, choose books, films or plays which are in some way related to the Literature course, if you are following one, so that you can keep your options open as to whether you present this assignment as part of your English or your English Literature coursework: it would be perfectly acceptable for both.

A review should be short, coherent and give a very clear impression of the kind of entertainment you can expect from the work you have chosen. You should begin (as in the review of *The Hobbit*) with a punchy first paragraph giving a brief but accurate idea of the overall feel of the work. You should then include a *succinct* plot summary (paragraph 2). The big temptation here is to go on for three pages telling the story, which will get you no marks at all: what is required is an assessment of how good the work is, not a simple account of its contents. You then go on to talk about specific aspects of the work that you enjoyed – in this case, individual scenes and characters – and include comments on the level of audience enjoyment (see paragraph 3). You should also mention shortcomings in sensible critical tones (paragraphs 4 and 5) but try to end on a positive note, as Jeremy Kingston does, perhaps leaving your readers with a specific picture or idea.

The Hobbit
The Fortune Theatre

Since this production contains the three essentials for a children's show – clear story, spectacular scenes and likeable heroes – the shortcomings a tetchy old grown-up 1 notices will not do much to diminish their enjoyment.

First the story. Well, it is Bilbo Baggins, the pint-sized Hobbit, shamed into joining 13 dwarves with jaw-crunching names in their fight to regain their ancestral territory. The journey is part treasure-hunt, part dragon-quest, undertaken by a reluctant Siegfried with hairy feet who discovers the thrilling terror of outwitting giant spiders 2 and crashing the skulls of evil goblins. He is helped by a benign wizard – and the lofty Dudley Long in his pointed hat alongside four-foot high Dixon make a quaintly attractive double-act.

The children I consulted did not mind the boring bits, the wordy or incomprehensible explanations. They had no sense of being cheated after the heroes are led away to 3 dungeons and nothing follows but the narrator's comment, 'don't worry – they escaped.' Tedious scenes and narrative cop-outs may even, I suppose, function as opportunities for a young audience to recover from the excitements elsewhere.

The first of these is a fight with luminous goblins, kitted out like spikey Siamese dancers, that culminates in the flight of a sword across the darkened stage. The decision to overlay Gollum's voice upon itself spoiled that encounter but momentum 4 picked up again with David Lumsden's excellent Beorn, rough and heavily moving like the bear he changes into.

High spot of the evening is the dragon Smaug, scaly and huge, on its nest of treasure. Impressively handled by a puppeteer below its neck, and speaking with the sarcastic George Sanders politeness expected of such beasts, it then comes forward 5 (four other puppeteers controlling its glittering wings) to stretch its neck across the orchestra pit and screech in rage before expiring like a collapsed pterodactyl.

(Review by Jeremy Kingston, *The Times*, Friday 12 December 1986)

LETTERS

There are a number of occasions, either in your coursework or in an Understanding paper, when you might have to present information in the form of a letter.

The ability to lay out a succinct and accurate letter is also something you will need to master very soon for job applications, letters of complaint or inquiry and many other purposes.

You write informal letters to your friends and family, in which the tone is familiar and personal, almost like a conversation. You write formal or business letters to people you do not know, to inquire about something, to apply for a job or about a course, to complain or ask for information. There are quite strict rules for the layout of a business letter. It should look like this:

Address & title of   *Your*
person to whom   *address*
letter is sent
                                  Date

Dear Sir/Madam or Dear Mr./Mrs./Miss
Reference Number (if applicable)

Yours faithfully or
Yours sincerely
Your signature

Your name printed
for clarity

Always write to someone using their name if you know it. If not, write 'Dear Sir', or 'Dear Madam'. If they hold a position such as 'Manager', you write that position on the first line of their address.

Make your letter as brief and to the point as possible.

Paragraph 1. Explain your reasons for writing.
Paragraph 2 onwards. The main body of the letter, where you put forward what you want to say in a clear, logical order, as politely as possible.
Conclusion. This should summarize the main purpose of the letter or say what the next stage in the correspondence should be.
Ending. This should be polite and include something like 'I look forward to hearing from you soon'.

Sign yourself 'Yours faithfully' if you began 'Dear Sir' or 'Dear Madam' and 'Yours sincerely' if you know the person's name.

Don't forget to print your name clearly under the signature.

A FINAL WORD ON EXPRESSION

The skills discussed in this chapter require time and consistent effort to perfect, as you cannot learn to write effectively overnight. Nor will simply thinking and talking about writing get you anywhere at all. The only way to achieve steady progress in your powers of expression is through constant practice in all the different areas, and this, above all, is what you should aim at in your course.

2. *Understanding English*

All the G C S E courses require you to read and understand as many different types of written material as possible. The examiners will expect you to be equally at home with stories, poems, plays, pieces of argumentative writing, advertisements, graphs, maps, diagrams, tables, charts, newspaper articles – in fact, anything and everything involving understanding written English. They are looking for the kind of reading skills that will get you through life successfully, not just through an examination, so the range of material you have to come to terms with on the course should be very wide.

This chapter is divided into three sections, each dealing with reading and understanding different types of 'English'. The sections are: Literary Material; Persuasive and Informative and Argumentative Writing; Factual, Diagrammatic and Pictorial Information. The chapter should help you to improve your reading skills and should also make you more aware of the number of different types of material you might meet in the Understanding section of your examination, if you are taking one.

THE LOGIC OF UNDERSTANDING

We'll begin with an exercise designed to tone you up for this section. Its purpose is to make you aware of the inner structure and logic of *any* piece of writing.

Every piece of writing has some kind of structure, as the writer has arranged material in order to make his or her point clear, to convey ideas and feelings with the maximum impact, or to communicate information as clearly and accurately as possible. Usually, paragraphs are connected together closely, and there is a logical progression through each paragraph.

This short newspaper item has been muddled up. Try to sort out its original order, by looking for clues in each paragraph which would link it to the next. Then turn over the page to see if you were correct.

Heads reject idea of 'model' English

1. Mr Kenneth Baker, the Education Secretary, wants the committee to try to find a "standard model" of the English language. But the country's largest head teachers' organisation, the National Association of Head Teachers, is to tell the committee that "in spoken English the association does not believe it to be possible or desirable to seek a 'standard model'."

3. The heads will also challenge other Government proposals and approaches on the teaching of English.

By John Fairhall,
Education Editor **2.**
Head teachers will today tell the Kingman committee – set up by the Education Secretary to report on how English should be taught – that one of its main objectives is wrong and impossible.

"It would be positively harmful **4.** in our view to start testing grammatical rules in any formal and regular way, particularly on a national basis at the ages of seven, 11 and 14," the NAHT says in the memorandum.

5. Some of Mr Baker's advisers have called for a return to the teaching of formal grammar in schools, and Mr Baker's Education Bill would establish national testing for all children at the ages of seven, 11 and 14 in English and other subjects.

6. "In written English we would hope for a clear indication from the committee that the accepted grammatical norms and structures of English are very important and necessary, but that they are not ends in themselves. Language is not acquired by learning rules first then applying them."

"It is far more important for **7.** pupils to be made aware of the variety of English usage in a social context and for their work to concentrate on developing appropriate (not standard) models for different situations," the NAHT says in a memorandum it has already submitted to the committee.

From *The Guardian.* Monday 13 July 1987

The correct order was:

2 . 1 . 7 . 3 . 5 . 4 . 6 .

Paragraph 2 introduces the topic (the NAHT's report to the Kingman committee) in one sentence, indicating the whole purpose of the article. Paragraph 1 expands on what the head teachers are reporting back to Mr Baker about the 'standard model' he has proposed. Paragraph 7 quotes from the memorandum concerning the standard model. Paragraph 3 (at the halfway point of the article) represents a change of subject and paragraph 5 goes on to the issue of formal grammar and is followed, again, by a quotation from the memorandum on this subject in paragraph 4. The final paragraph is an expansion of the point made in paragraph 4 and ends on a suitably definite note: 'Language is not acquired by learning rules first then applying them.'

Introduction: Head teachers report back to the Kingman committee on proposals made by Mr Baker for the Education Bill $\rightarrow$ The head teachers' comments on the 'standard model'
$\downarrow$
Expansion of their comments
$\downarrow$
Change of subject (short linking paragraph)
$\downarrow$

The head teachers' comments on this proposal $\leftarrow$ Mr Baker's plans for national testing in formal grammar at ages 7, 11, 14
$\downarrow$
Expansion of the comments

This is not an easy passage, and if you got the answer exactly right, give yourself a pat on the back. The exercise illustrates the point that to be fully aware of what we are reading and to understand how a passage works or why it is successful we need to be making judgements constantly, and to be alert to what a writer may be trying to say to us. We should never, ever, read carelessly, with one eye on the TV or both ears tuned in to the Walkman. A drop in concentration, and you have missed the sentence that links two points of an argument. (Remember how closely argued Orwell's article on Christmas was?) In everything you read, whether literary or non-literary, there is a logic and structure. It is up to you to find it.

UNDERSTANDING AND RESPONDING TO LITERARY MATERIAL

During your GCSE course, or in your examination, you will be given many pieces of literary material to read and understand – the extracts could be from novels, stories or plays, or you could be given a poem to look at. There are a number of things you need to do to prove to your teacher or examiner that you have understood and responded to them and the questions will be designed to test this.

First of all, you must understand both the *content* of the passage and its significance. Then, you need to be aware of the writer's *style* and his use of *language*. Finally, you are required to think about the ways in which the *writer's attitudes* emerge through his writing.

Let's begin by considering how you might approach a passage in order to come to a full understanding of its meaning and to respond to it in an individual way.

Breaking the Code

When you are faced with an extract from a book or play, or a poem, read it through very slowly and carefully with the main purpose of *understanding* it on a basic level, of seeing what is happening. Keep a completely open mind here because sometimes things may not be all they seem and you might have to do some quick rethinking of your expectations, as in the following opening paragraph from a novel, where the writer really plunges us in at the deep end:

I have no idea of the extent of this zoo. I know only my corner and whatever passes before me. On the day I was wheeled in, I only noticed two gates opening to admit me. When I stood up I caught a glimpse of some cages ahead and also heard the voice of a lion.

(*A Tiger for Malgudi* by R. K. Narayan)

There are certain clues in the passage as to the speaker's identity: 'voice' rather than 'roar'; 'wheeled in'; 'my corner'. The narrator has difficulty in seeing things, too, and very soon you realize that this is not a human being telling the story, as might be expected, but a tiger. Decoding clues like this is something we do almost automatically, and is all part of the process of understanding.

The *first reading* is also the time to check that you understand the words the writer is using, and you should underline any words you're unfamiliar with. You should also be trying to judge the *mood* or *tone* of the passage, getting its 'feel', so that you can respond to it. This will become apparent very quickly from the writer's choice of words as well as subject matter. In the following extract, the mood is immediately obvious, one of terror and a fear of the unknown. The *tone* is that of personal recollection by a narrator who remembers the incident with frightening accuracy:

I . . . dreamt again; if possible, still more disagreeably than before.

This time, I remembered I was lying in the oak closet, and I heard distinctly the gusty wind, and the driving of the snow; I heard, also, the fir-bough repeat its tearing sound, and ascribed it to the right cause; but it annoyed me so much, that I resolved to silence it, if possible; and, I thought, I rose and endeavoured to unhasp the casement. The hook was soldered into the staple, a circumstance observed by me when awake, but forgotten.

'I must stop it, nevertheless,' I muttered, knocking my knuckles through the glass and stretching an arm out to seize the importunate branch; instead of which, my fingers closed on the fingers of a little, ice-cold hand!

The intense horror of nightmare came over me; I tried to draw back my arm, but the hand clung to it, and a most melancholy voice sobbed,

'Let me in – let me in!'

(*Wuthering Heights* by Emily Brontë)

In the next extract (which we'll come back to shortly) the tone and mood are both much more difficult to pin down:

It is a truth universally acknowledged, that a single man in possession of a good fortune, must be in want of a wife.

However little known the feelings or views of such a man may be on his first entering a neighbourhood, this truth is so well fixed in the minds of the surrounding families, that he is considered as the rightful property of some one or other of their daughters.

(*Pride and Prejudice* by Jane Austen)

Glossary: Must be in want of: 'must need'

This brings us to our *second reading*, which should be much more searching than the first. Now, you should be *listening* to the passage, as you would imagine the author reading it, in order to get the full impact of particular words and to see the characters as individuals. You should be looking for all the ingredients of a piece of writing which we discussed in chapter 1: characters, description, atmosphere, use of dialogue, creation of suspense, point of view and interesting use of language. You should also be asking yourself, again, what is the *tone* of the passage, and that is what we'll now consider.

Let's consider the author's tone of voice in that second extract again. In the first sentence, Jane Austen seems to be putting forward an opinion, that 'a single man . . . must be in want of a wife'. But if you imagine her actually *saying* this, it becomes obvious that there is a slightly mocking tone, here. This is not her opinion at all, but 'a truth universally acknowledged'. It is what other people think, and Jane Austen doesn't necessarily share their views. If you think again, you have to question 'universally'. Surely everyone in the world doesn't think this? Does the young man himself believe it? The obvious conclusion is that Jane Austen is poking fun at the people who think this; it is *they* who assume that this is 'a truth universally acknowledged'. The writer doesn't agree with them, and in fact thinks they are a bit of a joke.

This type of writing, where the author seems to be saying one thing, but is in reality saying something quite different, is called irony. It is a very powerful weapon with which a writer can criticize people and what they think, as well as making us smile. Obviously, it is vitally important that you are on the alert for possible ironies in a passage to avoid badly misunderstanding the author's intentions.

So, your second reading should make you aware of the finer points of characterization, description, atmosphere, dialogue, suspense and use of language. You should also be looking more closely at the author's tone.

Your *third reading* – and remember, you haven't even looked at the questions yet – should allow you to come to grips with the passage's *style*: with such things as descriptive use of language, dialect, slang or dialogue. You should also look up or work out the meanings of unfamiliar words.

By this stage in your school career you should have invested in a good dictionary. Your teacher will advise you as to the best available. You should learn how to use it efficiently, and always have it to hand when you are reading. However, there are times when you will not have a dictionary handy, so it is sensible to have some idea of how to work out the meanings of words without it.

Look at the *Wuthering Heights* extract again. At a first reading, you may have underlined the following words: endeavoured, unhasp, casement, soldered, staple and importunate. Even with six words that you have never seen before, you should not have had any difficulty in working out what is actually taking place in the passage, so with this knowledge it should be possible to work out the meanings of the unfamiliar words.

'I rose and endeavoured to unhasp the casement.' This sounds very difficult but we very soon realize what the narrator is doing, if we look back over the passage. He has been listening to a fir-bough tapping (on a window, we gather) and he wants to 'silence' it. To do so, he would need to open the window. So we gather that 'casement' is an old-fashioned word for 'window' and 'unhasp' must mean 'undo'. As he still has not succeeded in opening the window – he has to break it – 'endeavoured' must mean 'tried'.

Then we need to ask ourselves why he might not have been able to open the window, to deduce what 'soldered' means: it becomes clear that the window's handle has been fixed immovably to the catch. 'Soldered', in fact, is what you do to two pieces of metal to fix them together permanently. Finally, 'importunate'. What had the branch been doing? It had seemed to be 'pleading' with him, and that is exactly what 'importunate' means.

Tackling the Questions

If you have read the passage three times, you are ready to begin on the questions. The kind of questions you might be asked could be divided in this way:

1. *Content and meaning*: what is happening and what are the *obvious* meanings of these events?
2. *Implications*: what are the hidden meanings behind what the writer has put down on paper? What does she want you to think and feel? What is the mood of the passage?
3. *Style*: what kind of writing is this? What kind of vocabulary does the writer use? How does she achieve her effects?
4. *Language*: Is the writer using language in an unusual or striking way?

5. *The writer's attitudes and opinions:* is she trying to persuade you to a certain point of view, or make you think a certain way?

In your answers to all these questions, the examiners will be looking for an ability to select the relevant material for each question, and to answer using a clear, direct style. They will also be looking for evidence of a personal response to the passage(s), an area we'll consider in greater detail later in the chapter.

Obviously, they will set slightly different sorts of question for prose, poetry and play extracts. In each type of writing, the author achieves his or her effects in a variety of ways, so you need to be looking out for a different set of signals in each case.

We'll now take a look at prose, poetry and drama passages in detail, to work out a method of understanding them. We'll then look at how some students tackled GCSE examination papers testing Understanding and Response to Literary Material. When you are studying question papers, you should keep a pencil handy and underline important words, phrases and significant details, as I have done with the prose extract that follows. You might also like to make notes in the margin, or on a separate sheet of paper, noting down your impressions of the passage.

Prose

Our prose passage is a description of a rain forest:

The shaded river seemed to offer relief from the sun but beneath the trees, the air was clogged with heat and full of the steamy effluvia of decay. Added to the wasps and bees, there were now mosquitoes. Though the transparent, quietly-moving stream made for easy going, there were obstructions here, too. Trees, brought down by lightning, lay across the water, their thick ligatures of creeper stretching like nets about them. In places the undergrowth reached out of its overcrowded environment to meet the undergrowth on the other side.

A grey-green twilight hung on the air with here and there a spot of sunlight lying like a coin on the water. They came into a region of romantic beauty where dragonflies

First paragraph:
heat
decay
insects
Difficult to get through.
Feeling of overcrowding.
Third-person narrator.
V. descriptive.

Second paragraph:
simile
colours
beauty
dragonflies replace other
insects.

Abundant life.
There are two people, one called Simon.

skimmed the river and the hanging creepers were in flower. The trees were grown over with ferns, orchids, moss and lichens. Some of the orchids were blue and some of the red and gold kind that Simon called Vallambrosa. As the stream narrowed and they made their way into a tunnel of gloom, the flowers were left behind. Here the fallen trees were white with age and bearded over with lichens.

Third paragraph:
Sense of mystery.
Identified as at least two men named Simon and Hugh.
Return to feeling of claustrophobia.

Closed in by trees, the men were assaulted by a whining, galactic army of wasps, bees, mosquitoes and tiny flies. The forest came so close that Hugh could peer between the interwoven branches and creepers but he saw only the inner darkness. He felt a nervous dread of the forest coming too close to him.

(The Rain Forest by Olivia Manning)

You notice at the *first reading* that there is no dialogue, that this is a purely descriptive passage in the third person. The storyteller seems to be following two characters on a journey as she refers to 'they', 'he', 'Simon' and 'Hugh' on a number of occasions. You also notice that the description is very dense, and that it seems to suggest a confused picture of the rain forest.

At the *second reading*, you become more aware of how the impression of the rain forest is created, and a very complex picture is emerging. On the one hand, the rain forest is full of horror, discomfort, unease and claustrophobia. You pick this feeling up from phrases such as 'clogged with heat', 'the steamy effluvia of decay', 'creeper stretching like nets', 'nervous dread' and 'inner darkness'. On the other hand, it is a magical region, full of unearthly beauty: 'a spot of sunlight lying like a coin on the water', 'romantic beauty', 'dragonflies', and 'flowers'.

You also see more clearly that the passage really seems to be about the impact the rain forest had on one particular character – Hugh. This point comes home in the final paragraph when the writer refers to his 'nervous dread of the forest coming too close to him'. At this point you realize that we are probably seeing the forest from his point of view, as in paragraph 1 the creeper is 'like nets', and this sounds very much like the kind of comparison someone would make if they were afraid of being enclosed and imprisoned.

On your *third reading*, the picture becomes even clearer. Your senses are assaulted by smells (of 'decay', orchids and heat) by sounds (of insects buzzing and the quiet murmur of the stream) and by sights (thick undergrowth, lush vegetation, various colours and contrasting darkness). You can also feel the enclosing creepers, the stinging insects. This accuracy and vividness is achieved through a direct appeal to the senses and a piling up of details.

You can pick out two similes (and if you are not sure about what a simile is, see p. 75): 'like nets' and 'like a coin on the water'. You can also follow through continual references to the fact that Hugh feels as if the forest is closing in around him: 'obstructions', 'like nets', 'overcrowded environment', 'narrowed', 'closed in', 'so close', 'too close'.

There are some difficult words. You may have underlined: effluvia, ligature, lichens, orchids, galactic. The meanings of these words are not too hard to get at. If you think of decay, it is not too hard to imagine that the writer is referring to a smell, and 'effluvia' looks a bit like 'flowing' so you can piece together the conclusion that the writer is describing a very bad smell 'flowing out' of the decay. The ligatures that she refers to are stretched around the trees, so they could be some kind of wrapping or bandage. The word 'lichens' is included in a list which also mentions ferns and moss, so we gather they are some kind of plant. Later on the orchids are described as 'red and gold' and 'blue', so they must be beautiful flowers. Finally, 'galactic' sounds like 'galaxy', and if you look up at the sky, there is a 'galaxy' of stars – thousands of them; so, you realize that the writer is trying to tell you what a huge number of the insects there were.

Now, let's have a look at how a student tackled a set of GCSE questions on prose, in timed conditions. We'll concentrate for the moment on the questions which test your understanding of the passage, your ability to appreciate its mood, style, and language, and your skill in selecting and reorganizing material to write clear and well-ordered answers. We'll come back later to the kind of question, which, as well as asking you to do all these things, also asks you to write expressively, using your own imagination. I have included the student's marginalia, to help you to see how she arrived at her answers.

Part I

Read the following passages. Both give accounts of teenagers meeting some old people. As you read, you should consider the following:

each person's behaviour, feelings and attitudes towards the old people;
the old people's feelings about them;
and the ways in which things are described.

You will be asked questions on these points in Part II.

You have fifteen minutes' reading time. You may make notes on details of the passages in your answer book.

After fifteen minutes you will be given **Part II**. *This will give you the questions to answer on the passages.*

Passage One

The person keeping the diary is Adrian Mole, aged 13¾.

Sunday July 4th.

FOURTH AFTER TRINITY.
AMERICAN INDEPENDENCE DAY.

I was just starting to eat my <u>Sunday</u> dinner when Bert Baxter rang and asked me to go round urgently. I bolted my spaghetti Bolognese down as quickly as I could and ran round to Bert's.

He comes round when they're in need

Sabre, the vicious Alsatian, was standing at the door looking worried. As a precaution I gave him a dog choc and hurried into the bungalow. Bert was sitting in the living room in his <u>wheelchair, the television was switched off so I know something serious had happened.</u> He said, 'Queenie's had a <u>bad turn'.</u> I went into the tiny bedroom. Queenie was lying in the big saggy bed looking gruesome (<u>she hadn't put her artificial cheeks or lips on</u>). She said, 'You're a good lad to come round, Adrian'. I asked her what was wrong. She said, 'I've been having pains like red hot needles in my chest.'

observant

Adrian's kindness

Bert interrupted, 'You said the pains were like red-hot knives five minutes ago!' *They're still getting at each other*

'Needles, knives, who cares?' she said.

I asked Bert if he had called the doctor. He said he hadn't because Queenie was frightened of doctors. I rang my mother and asked her advice. She said she'd come round. *old fashioned*

sensible

While we waited for her I made a cup of tea and fed Sabre and made Bert a beetroot sandwich. *kind and practical*

My mother and father came and took over. My mother phoned for an ambulance. It was a good job they did because while it was coming Queenie went a bit strange and started talking about ration books and stuff. *frightening, although funny*

Bert held her hand and called her a 'daft old bat.' *affection*

The ambulance men were just shutting the doors when Queenie shouted out, 'Fetch me pot of rouge, I'm not going until I've got me rouge.' I ran into the bedroom and looked on the dressing table. The top was covered in pots and hair nets and hairpins and china dishes and lace mats and photos of babies and weddings. I found the rouge in a little drawer and took it to Queenie. My mother went off in the ambulance and me and my father stayed behind to comfort Bert. Two hours later my mother rang from the hospital to say that Queenie had had a stroke and would be in hospital for ages. *again – generous*

Bert said, 'What am I going to do without my girl to help me!'

Girl! Queenie is seventy-eight. *Adrian is still detached*

Bert wouldn't come home with us. He is scared that the council will take his bungalow away from him. *touching*

Thursday July 29th *over three weeks later*

My father has been working flat out on the canal bank for the past three days. He hasn't been getting home until 10 p.m. at night. He is getting dead neurotic about leaving it and going on holiday.

Went to see Queenie in hospital. She is in a ward full of old ladies with sunken white faces. It's a good *observant* *kind to visit her* *horrific*

job that Queenie was wearing her rouge, I wouldn't
have recognised her without it.

Queenie can't speak properly so it was dead   Adrian is sorry for
embarrassing trying to work out what she was saying.   them
I left after twenty minutes, worn out with smiling. I
tried not to look at the old ladies as I walked back
down the ward, but it didn't stop them shouting out
to me and waving. One of them asked me to fetch a
nice piece of cod for her husband's tea. The tired-
looking nurse said that a lot of the old ladies were
living in the past. I can't say I really blame them; their
present is dead horrible.

nearly two months
later Sunday September 19th

FIFTEENTH AFTER TRINITY

not long really Took a deep breath and went to see Bert and
Queenie today. They were hostile to me because I've
neglected them for a week.

Bert said, 'He's not bothered about us old 'uns no
more, Queenie. He's more interested in gadding
about.'

very human How unfair can you get? I can't remember the last
time I gadded about. Queenie didn't say anything
because she can't speak properly because of the
stroke, but she certainly looked antagonistic.

Adrian doesn't
really object Bert ordered me to come back tomorrow to clean
up. Their home help comes on Tuesdays and Bert
likes the place to be tidy for when she comes.

about 6 weeks
later Sunday November 7th

Went to see Bert and Queenie with my mother.

Everyone we met on the way asked my mother
when the baby was due, or made comments like, 'I
expect you'll be glad when the baby's here, won't
you?'

My mother was very ungracious in her replies.

Bert opened the door, he said, 'Ain't you dropped
that sprog yet?'

humorous My mother said, 'Shut your mouth, you clapped-
out geriatric.'

Honestly, sometimes I long for bygone days, when people spoke politely to each other. You would never guess that my mother and Bert are fond of each other.

Everyone was too old, or too ill, or too pregnant to do any cooking (I developed a sudden ache in both wrists). So we ate bread and cheese for our Sunday dinner. Then, in the afternoon we took it in turns to teach Queenie to speak again.

Again, Adrian is kind to her

I got her to say, 'A jar of beetroot please', dead clearly. I might be a speech therapist when I grow up. I have got a definite flair for it. We got a taxi back home because my mother's ankles got a bit swollen. The taxi driver moaned because the distance was only half a mile.

Passage Two

Winter

It was mid-morning – a very cold, bright day. Holding a potted plant before her, a girl of fourteen jumped off the bus in front of the Old Ladies' Home, on the outskirts of town. She wore a red coat and her straight yellow hair hanging down loose from the pointed white cap all the little girls were wearing that year. She stopped for a moment beside one of the prickly dark shrubs with which the city had beautified the Home, and then proceeded slowly toward the building, which was of whitewashed brick and reflected the winter sunlight like a block of ice. As she walked vaguely up the steps she shifted the small pot from hand to hand; then she had to set it down and remove her mittens before she could open the heavy door.

She's some kind of Brownie

It sounds rather unpleasant

a sinister simile

'I'm a Campfire Girl . . . I have asked to pay a visit to some old lady', she told the nurse at the desk. This was a woman in a white uniform who looked as if she were cold; she had close-cut hair which stood up on

She's just going to gain points: no other motive

everything is cold

the very top of her head exactly like a sea wave. Marian, the little girl, did not tell her that this visit would give her a minimum of only three points in her score.

'Acquainted with any of our residents?' asked the nurse. She lifted one eyebrow and spoke like a man.

'With any old ladies? No – but – that is, any of them will do,' Marian stammered. With her free hand she pushed her hair behind her ears, as she did when it was time to study Science.

The nurse shrugged and rose. 'You have a nice multiflora cineraria there,' she remarked as she walked ahead down the hall of closed doors to pick out an old lady.

> impersonal

There was loose, bulging linoleum on the floor. Marian felt as if she were walking on the waves, but the nurse paid no attention to it. There was a smell in the hall like the interior of a clock. Everything was silent until, behind one of the doors, an old lady of some kind cleared her throat like a sheep bleating. This decided the nurse. Stopping in her tracks, she first extended her arm, bent her elbow, and leaned forward from the hips – all to examine the watch strapped to her wrist; then she gave a loud double-rap on the door.

> sensory details

> The nurse is im-personal

'There are two in each room,' the nurse remarked over her shoulder.

'Two what?' asked Marian without thinking. The sound like a sheep's bleating almost made her turn around and run back.

> she's getting scared

One old woman was pulling the door open in short, gradual jerks, and when she saw the nurse a strange smile forced her face dangerously awry. Marian, suddenly propelled by the strong impatient arm of the nurse, saw next the side-face of another old woman, even older, who was lying flat in bed with a cap on and a counterpane drawn up to her chin.

> horrifying

> nurse like a man

'Visitor,' said the nurse, and after one more shove she was off down the hall.

Marian stood tongue-tied; both hands held the potted plant. The old woman, still with that terrible,

> The old woman is doing her best

square smile (which was a smile of welcome) stamped on her bony face, was waiting . . . Perhaps she said something. The old woman in bed said nothing at all, and she did not look around.

Suddenly Marian saw a hand, quick as a bird claw, reach up to the air and pluck the white cap off her head. At the same time another claw to match drew her all the way into the room, and the next moment the door closed behind her.

It suddenly turns nasty

unpleasant simile

'My, my, my,' said the old lady at her side.

Marian stood enclosed by a bed, a washstand and a chair, the tiny room had altogether too much furniture. Everything smelled wet – even the bare floor. She held on to the back of the chair which was wicker and felt soft and damp. Her heart beat more and more slowly, her hands got colder and colder, and she could not hear whether the old women were saying anything or not. She could not see them very clearly. How dark it was! The window blind was down, and the only door was shut. Marian looked at the ceiling . . . It was like being caught in a robbers' cave, just before one was murdered.

Perhaps she just wants to look at her hair

Everything becomes frightening

she thinks it's like a story

Part II

The questions which follow are based on the passages given to you in **Part I.** *Using only the information you have gained from reading these passages,* **answer questions 1–5.** The five questions carry equal marks.

You may make any further notes to help you in your answer book. Cross out all your notes when you have answered all the questions.

Passage One

1. Describe in detail Queenie's 'turn' and what happens to her afterwards.
2. What do you learn about Adrian Mole's behaviour, feelings and attitude towards Bert and Queenie from the way he treats them?

Passage Two

3. What impressions are given of the atmosphere and conditions of the Old Ladies' Home?
4. Imagine that Marian keeps a diary. Write her diary entry for the day she visits the

Home. Include the important things that she notices and what she feels about them. Bear in mind that a diary entry need not be too long (see Adrian Mole's).

Both Passages
5. Imagine that you are an elderly person reading these two passages. Give your impression of the two young people involved.

(LEAG GCSE English Specimen Paper 1988)

This examination paper asks you to examine two completely different prose extracts, which are linked thematically, as they both centre around an old ladies' ward or home. As you can see, the extracts are quite long, so you would need to take your time, examining them. Remember that you should have a pencil in your hand, to underline words and phrases which you think are important, and to make notes. You are given fifteen minutes' reading time and the rubric (that is, the instructions at the beginning of the examination) advises you to 'make notes on details of the passages in your answer book'.

There are very few questions, so your answers should be full and accurate. Always look to see how many marks each question is worth, as this will tell you how much detail is required in your answer. There is no need, ever, to rush, as the allowance of time is generous. During your reading time, you *must* underline and make notes of the main details of the passage, using the method already demonstrated.

For question 1, you would need to include as many of the details about the 'turn' included in the passage as possible:

Queenie's 'turn' was really a stroke and in the first entry of the diary, Adrian describes how she was confined to her bed with sharp pains in her chest. This must have been the beginning of her stroke. She was obviously very ill because she was described as wearing no make-up which was quite unusual for her. Next, she started to become delirious and this explains her being described as 'strange' and talking about ration books. She was then taken to hospital in an ambulance and must have had a very serious stroke there. Twenty-five days later, we are told that Queenie was still in hospital in a very serious condition because she couldn't speak at all. About two months later, we are told that she was back at home, but still couldn't say anything. By Sunday, November 7th, she was starting to learn how to say short sentences, so was beginning to recover slowly.

Lola included all the relevant details from the passage. She also used the dates of the diary extracts to convey the impression that she was aware of the passage of time during Queenie's illness. This shows that she was making full use of the passage. She used her own words, which is something you should always do. The examiners are not looking for your ability to quote from the passage.

The second question requires you to think about the *implications* of Adrian Mole's behaviour. You can't just write up the relevant bits from the passage, you need to think about the meanings behind them, using your powers of analysis. This was Lola's answer:

When Bert Baxter rang, Adrian came to his bungalow as fast as possible, which means that he felt some responsibility for him. When he discovered that Queenie was ill he checked whether a doctor had been called and on discovering that one hadn't, he rang his mother for advice instead. He must have felt genuinely anxious about Queenie and showed kindness for the two old people by doing little household jobs and making some quick food.

Later, when Queenie was being put in the ambulance, it was he who fetched her rouge which proves that he must have respected her feelings, although he was amused. Later he stayed with Bert to comfort him, showing some concern, and he offered that Bert should come home with him – even though he can't possibly have wanted him to.

Adrian probably visited Queenie in hospital partly out of a sense of duty, but there must also have been some kind thought in this gesture: he could have made excuses. Although he only stayed with Queenie 20 minutes, which shows that of course he didn't enjoy being with her in that condition, he made an effort not to hurt her feelings and so kept on smiling.

We also discover in the next extract that although he likes Bert and Queenie, and cares about them, he doesn't often enjoy visiting them and does so when his conscience tells him to rather than of his own free will. On this particular visit he must have hated coming to see them and felt angry at being told that he 'gadded about'. These feelings were probably mixed with a little bit of guilt that he hadn't visited them for a week.

In the last extract, Adrian visited Bert and Queenie with his mother, probably because he didn't mind seeing them so much with his mother as well. Neither he nor his mother did any cooking because they were too lazy. The fact that it would be a kind gesture to cook a meal for two old people did not seem to affect him – and this is very human. However, no one seemed to mind eating bread and cheese, which shows that there was a real affection between them all, instead of just a formal relationship between helper and helped.

Adrian probably helped to teach Queenie to speak partly because it was fun and a novelty – something he enjoyed doing rather than an act of charity.

In conclusion, I think that Adrian liked Bert and Queenie, rather than treating them simply as people to be helped. But he would not always enjoy visiting them and would do so because he thought it was his duty to do so. So, his feelings were quite a complex mixture of love, impatience and a sense of duty.

She has completely taken to pieces every single thing that Adrian does or thinks in connection with the Baxters, and the result is a thorough and sensitive piece of writing. She has made eighteen points, and each action or thought is very carefully considered. It is an excellent answer, and would gain a very high mark.

Question 3 requires you to track down all the descriptive details in the second passage, and put them together to give a full account of the extract's success as a piece of atmospheric and descriptive writing. Again, a fairly lengthy answer was required.

The building of the Old Ladies' Home was whitewashed, with a few shrubs outside. This suggested to me that someone had tried to make the outside look pretty and inviting whereas the inside would not be beautiful at all. This misleading appearance of the outside would make people think that the inside kept up to the same standard and the old women were treated well as they were living in good conditions. However, the inside of the Home appears to be rather frightening and cold with its long hall of closed doors. There seems to be no life or any sign of the old ladies doing any activities in the home, but they all appear to be locked up in the rooms. The 'loose, bulging linoleum' and the smell of 'the interior of a clock' all add to the impression of a shut-up, unhappy mental asylum or prison.

The silence suggests no enjoyment among the old ladies, like talking among each other or playing any kind of games. It seems as if they are all ill or confined separately – again like a prison. The conditions of the rooms are definitely not up to the standard they should have been for an Old Ladies' Home. The rooms should have been bright and cheerful, with perhaps flowers and pictures, not dark and obviously suffering from damp on the walls, which would definitely affect an old lady's health. The bare floor might have been much more pleasant for the old women if there had been a carpet and there should have been more light in the bedroom during the day so maybe curtains would have been better than a blind. The whole atmosphere is cold and cheerless for an old ladies' home. It greatly resembles a prison to punish the inmates and not a happy and comforting place where old people can die peacefully.

Again, Lola has successfully absorbed all the descriptive details included in the passage and she draws a conclusion from each. She also seems to have responded sensitively to the unpleasantness of the atmosphere and suggests what is disturbing and unattractive about the home. So, she gives the impression of having been attentive to the mood of the passage as well as its contents. She takes trouble to make more general comments, too, on the overall picture of the home.

We'll consider questions 4 and 5 later in the separate sub-section on Using your Imagination (pp. 90–95).

Poetry

Let's suppose that you have been given a poem in the examination and consider how to approach it. 'Breaking the code' of a poem is different from prose or a play, but don't be put off by poetry. It has a language of its own which you need to learn, as you would any other language, and this requires time and effort.

Facing Up to a Poem

You should give a poem the same three searching readings we have discussed already, but there are certain things happening in a poem that don't happen in a novel or a play, and you need to be paying attention to those as well.

The Shape of a Poem

First of all, a poem is arranged on the page in a certain way. It may be broken up into verses (or 'stanzas') and the poet will be making use of rhythm and perhaps of rhyme.

The poem's arrangement on the page is called its 'form'. There are many different ways in which a poet can say what he wants to say and he will choose the form he feels is most suitable for it. For instance, this poet has chosen to make considerable use of rhyme and it gives the poem an air of order and finality:

> *Into my heart an air that kills*
> *From yon far country blows:*
> *What are those blue remembered hills,*
> *What spires, what farms are those?*
>
> *That is the land of lost content,*
> *I see it shining plain,*
> *The happy highways where I went*
> *And cannot come again.*

> ('Blue Remembered Hills' by
> A. E. Housman)

You can see that the verse-form is very strict: the first and third and the second and fourth lines of each stanza rhyme and both stanzas are four lines long and have the same number of beats: four in lines 1 and 3, three in lines 2 and 4. Housman uses the rhyme to press his points home to us and the poem's impact is very definite. We get a clear impression of a loss of childhood innocence, and a sense of deep sadness.

The next poet has chosen to write 'free verse', that is, verse with no regular scheme of rhythm and rhyme, unlike A. E. Housman's poem. He uses rhyme where he wants to and makes the lines long or short according to the impact he is trying to create. Generally, free verse has a more conversational tone – it sounds as if the poet is sharing his thoughts with you:

> *And I saw the horses:*
>
> *Huge in the dense grey – ten together –*
> *Megalith-still. They breathed, making no move,*
>
> *With draped manes and tilted hind-hooves,*
> *Making no sound.*
>
> *I passed: not one snorted or jerked its head.*
> *Grey silent fragments*
>
> *Of a grey silent world.*

('The Horses' by Ted Hughes)

Hughes uses the verse-form to try to re-create for us his vividly remembered experience of seeing the horses. The poem's shape imitates the different stages of the experience and the free-flowing, unrestricted verse matches the poem's reflective mood.

So, always be attentive to the form of a poem and the way the poet is using that form.

Language

You will have noticed already that poets often use language in a surprising and unusual way – much more frequently than the writer of a novel or play. They seem to use similes, metaphors and personification more often, and they make much more use of the *sounds* of words. This is because a poem is, generally, much more compact than a story or play, and poets have to pack in as much meaning as possible.

Let's look at a few examples of how poets make interesting uses of the sounds and meanings of the words they choose.

SIMILE

A simile is a direct comparison usually introduced by the words 'like' or 'as'. The poet uses a simile to express more clearly *his* way of looking at something and often the comparison may be very surprising. The following poet has an unusual way of looking at washing on a line:

> *In the dusk of a garden fagged by the* electric day,
> *Pale washing hung beyond the blackening roses*
> Shifts like restless visitors who cannot get away.

('A House in Summer' by James Kirkup)

Here, the poet is comparing washing on a line to visitors who are trying to 'escape'. This simile conveys a clear picture of the washing pulling wearily at the line, in the breeze. A simile is a very condensed way of conveying ideas.

METAPHOR

A metaphor is an *indirect* comparison. There is no 'like' or 'as' but you can recognize a metaphor when you spot a word that seems to be describing something in terms of something else. For instance, if you wrote that 'the teacher growled at the pupil', you know that a teacher can't growl in the way a dog growls: what you are suggesting is that the sound the teacher made in anger was very like the sound an angry dog makes. In other words, you are *indirectly* comparing an angry teacher to an angry dog. So 'growled' is a *metaphorical* use of the word.

If you look back at the previous extract, you will see that there is a metaphor there, too, in the phrase 'electric day'. After all, a day can't really be electric: the poet is telling us that the day was very bright, painfully hot, and full of tension (perhaps there is going to be a storm?).

You will find far more metaphors and similes in poetry than in prose. They make us think more carefully about things, and one metaphor may suggest many other areas of comparison.

PERSONIFICATION

A poet uses personification when he gives an object, an animal, a natural event or an abstract idea human characteristics. In the following extract the poet sees death as a person who is less threatening than you might imagine:

> *Death be not proud, though some have called thee*
> *Mighty and dreadfull, for thou art not soe.*

(from one of John Donne's 'Divine Poems')

Again, such a poetic technique expands and deepens our understanding of what the poet is saying. These lines help us to see death in a completely different light.

THE SOUNDS OF WORDS

You will find that poets constantly make use of the *sounds* of words to make the pictures they are creating in our minds as clear as they possibly can. There are different ways in which they can get the most out of the sounds of words.

One of the most frequently used of these techniques is *onomatopoeia*, where the sound of a word echoes its meaning exactly, as in the line

> *The shooting surf comes hissing round.*

('Greenaway' by John Betjeman)

where the use of the letter 's' helps us to *hear* the sound of the sea's waves. Other onomatopoeiac words include 'crack' and 'buzz'.

Often, too, poets repeat certain letters in a line or lines to create a specific atmosphere. For instance, in the following lines the repetition of the letter 'w' suggests the 'whooshing' sound of the wind that the poet is trying to convey:

> *The wind blew all my wedding-day,*
> *And my wedding-night was the night of the high wind.*

('Wedding Night' by Philip Larkin)

This type of repetition of consonants is called *alliteration* and you will find it in many of the poems you read.

Assonance is very like alliteration, except that *vowel sounds* rather than consonant-sounds are repeated, as in the following line

> *Weeded and worn the ancient thatch*
> *Upon the lonely moated grange.*

('Mariana' by Alfred, Lord Tennyson)

where the repetition of the moaning 'o' sounds suggests sadness and loneliness.

Both assonance and alliteration increase our enjoyment of poetry, especially when it is read aloud.

Let's have a look at a poem in detail, trying to come to a full understanding of the poet's meaning through our three readings, paying special attention to the poem's form and looking out for simile, metaphor, personification, alliteration and assonance (but remember you may come across a number of poems where you won't be able to find any of these techniques).

The Meadow Mouse

I

In a shoe box stuffed in an old nylon stocking
Sleeps the baby mouse I found in the meadow,
Where he trembled and shook beneath a stick
Till I caught him up by the tail and brought him in,
Cradled in my hand,
A little quaker, the whole body of him trembling,
His absurd whiskers sticking out like a cartoon-mouse,
His feet like small leaves,
Little lizard-feet,
Whitish and spread wide when he tried to struggle away,
Wriggling like a minuscule puppy.

Now he's eaten his three kinds of cheese and drunk from his bottle-cap
  watering-trough –
So much he just lies in one corner,
His tail curled under him, his belly big
As his head, his bat-like ears
Twitching, tilting toward the least sound.

Do I imagine he no longer trembles
When I come close to him?
He seems no longer to tremble.

II

But this morning the shoe-box house on the back porch is empty.
Where has he gone, my meadow mouse,
My thumb of a child *that nuzzled in my palm? –*

To run under the hawk's wing,
Under the eye of the great owl watching from the elm-tree,
To live by courtesy of the shrike, the snake, the tom-cat.

I think of the nestling fallen into the deep grass,
The turtle gasping in the dusty rubble of the highway,
The paralytic stunned in the tub, and the water rising, –
All things innocent, hapless, forsaken.

(Theodore Roethke)

This poem is very moving and has a feeling of immediacy which certainly comes from personal experience. It is divided into two sections and is in free verse – the poet does not make use of rhyme. This free-flowing form allows him to give the impression that he is expressing his feelings by talking to us directly.

The first section consists of three stanzas (verses) of different lengths. In the *first stanza*, the poet describes how he found the mouse and brought it home. He uses similes (underlined) to give us a clear picture of the mouse. He also makes use of alliteration in the lines, 'Whitish and spread wide when he tried to struggle away,/Wriggling like a minuscule puppy'. In the *second stanza*, he describes the mouse asleep after a big meal, and the description makes us feel protective towards the mouse – in other words, we are made to share the poet's feelings. Again, he uses alliteration in the line, 'Twitching, tilting . . .' to stress the mouse's nervousness. The *third stanza* suggests the poet's desire to make friends with the mouse.

Then, there is a clear break in the poem, marking the one night for which the poet left the mouse. The second section consists of two stanzas and describes the next morning when he finds the box empty. In the *fourth stanza*, he thinks of the mouse in danger from predators. Its tiny size is stressed in the metaphor, 'My thumb of a child' – it is only as big as a child's finger. In the *final stanza*, he thinks of all the other helpless creatures in the world, who might die innocently at any time. It is a very moving final stanza. The mouse has become a symbol of all the innocent suffering that the poet has seen or heard about in the world.

We'll move on, now, to look at how one student tackled the questions on a poem on a specimen GCSE paper.

EXAMPLE A

Read the following poem and then answer the questions below.

Hide and Seek

First-person

Call out. Call loud: 'I'm ready! Come and find
  me!'
The sacks in the toolshed smell like the seaside.

Sensory details

They'll never find me in this salty dark,

Child's point of → But be careful that your feet aren't sticking out.
view
Wiser not to risk another shout.

Use of rhyme

The floor is cold. They'll probably be searching
The bushes near the swing. Whatever happens
You mustn't sneeze when they come prowling in.
And here they are, whispering at the door;

Immediacy

You've never heard them sound so hushed
  before.   10

Effective: long line

Don't breathe. Don't move. Stay dumb. Hide in
  your blindness.
They're moving closer, someone stumbles,
  mutters;

Present tense

Their words and laughter scuffle and they're
  gone.
But don't come out just yet; they'll try the lane,

It's all going on in

And then the greenhouse and back here again.

his mind – he's

They must be thinking that you're very clever,

imagining them

Getting more puzzled as they search all over.

Poem changes

It seems a long time since they went away.

assonance – eerie

Your legs are stiff, the cold bites through your
  coat;
The dark damp smell of sand moves in your
  throat.   20

He's still deter-
mined

It's time to let them know that you're the winner.
Push off the sacks. Uncurl and stretch. That's

Uncomfortable

  better!
Out of the shed and call to them 'I've won!'
'Here I am! Come and own up I've caught you!'

Creepy

The darkening garden watches. Nothing stirs.
The bushes hold their breath; the sun is gone.

He hasn't won

Yes, here you are. But where are they who

Has he grown up?

sought you?

Vernon Scannell

Section A

Answer **all** *the following questions.*

(a) Choose details from the first part of the poem to show how Vernon Scannell is trying to build up a clear picture of the shed and of being in hiding.   (3)

(b) How does the person in hiding come to realise that it is time to give up?   (3)

(c) Although it is written in one piece, the poem can be said to be in two parts. Say where the change or 'break' in the poem comes and, in your own words, show how the parts are different.   (6)

(d) In your own words, express clearly what is being described by:
    'Hide in your blindness' (line 11).   (2)
    and
    'The dark, damp smell of sand moves in your throat' (line 20).   (2)

(e) Does the poem gain by being written in the present tense (as if it is happening now)? Refer to the poem in your answer.   (5)

(f) At the end, the writer makes it clear that the others have left the garden. How exactly does he do this?   (4)

(g) Could the writer be trying to do more than describe an experience from childhood? Look at the poem again, and write about what the last line suggests to you. Write no more than 80 words.   (5)

(Total 30 marks)

Section B

Choose **one** *of the following.*

You may write in playscript, poetry or prose. If you write in playscript, just put the speaker's name in the left margin, and then the words spoken. Remember that credit will be given for your ability to describe scenes, people, thoughts and feelings, and for your choice of words.

You should write between 200–250 words.

1 Imagine you are the person in the poem, and that you have found your friends again. Describe what happens, how you behave and what is said.

OR

2 Put yourself in the place of one of the searchers.
Describe your feelings as you look into the shed. Write about what happens next.

(30 marks)

(MEG GCSE English Specimen Paper 1986)

This Understanding question paper involves detailed study of a modern poem in free verse. Questions a) and b) check that you have understood what is happening in the poem:

a) Vernon Scannell is trying to build up a clear picture of the shed and being in hiding by using lines such as:
'. . . I'm ready, come and find me'.
Almost immediately we can tell that this is a child's game of hide-and-seek and this sets the picture for the rest of the poem. The line:
'The sacks in the toolshed smell like the seaside'
conveys a picture of a dark shed used for storage in which the child has decided to hide. This line very quickly builds up a picture of the shed and the image of the child being in hiding is strengthened by the next line:
'They'll never find me in this salty dark.'
The child's point of view and ideas are shown in:
'But be careful that your feet aren't sticking out',
'You mustn't sneeze when they come prowling in' and
'Don't breathe, don't move . . .'
We can easily imagine the child hiding in the dark shed and just beginning to feel uncomfortable in lines such as:
'The floor is cold'.

Kate picks out all the details which give the clearest impression of the shed and she also notices that the shed is very much seen from the child's point of view. Her answer to b) was equally thorough:

b) The person in hiding comes to realise that it is time to give up when he starts to feel cramped, cold and uncomfortable in the toolshed:
'Your legs are stiff, the cold bites through your coat'.
He is also probably beginning to feel bored, is looking forward to crowing over his friends and realizes from past experience that they will soon become tired of looking for him, and will be relieved when he finally shows himself. We can see this from:
'It seems a long time since they went away' and
'It's time to let them know that you're the winner'.

Question c) was a little more difficult. It required you to notice that a long time has gone by since the others left and the poet says 'It seems a long time since they went away'. You had to show your responsiveness to the different moods of the two parts of the poem:

c) I feel that the change or 'break' in the poem comes at the line
'It seems a long time since they went away'.
The parts are different in so far as leading up to the break there have been a few lines which all rhyme, and this line comes as a non-rhyming one which is a surprise. It has an almost sinister effect on the poem. The first half seems like a game, like the author's childhood experiences, but the second half of the poem, particularly the last few lines, seem to have a deeper meaning than just a childhood game, and become much less lighthearted. Scannell uses more 'adult' metaphors such as 'the bushes hold their breath', and thoughts which are not used in the first part of the poem. It almost sounds as if between the first and second halves of the poem, the poet has grown up.

Kate has responded to the changed mood of the poem, its sinister overtones and its suggestion of movement from childhood to the adult world.

Question d) asked you to analyse certain phrases very precisely. Kate's answer was accurate and clear:

d) 'Hide in your blindness'.
To me this seems to convey that the child has camouflaged himself so well that he cannot see out from his hiding place, but can hear the footsteps, and hides, unseeing.
'The dark, damp smell of sand moves in your throat'.
This, to me means that the child has been in the toolshed for quite a long time, the smell in there is beginning to become too much for him and is going to make him cough. If he coughs, he will probably be found anyway, and this could be another factor in his decision to give himself up and still have the glory of winning.

Question e) was looking for some analysis of what is 'present' rather than 'past' about the poem. You would need to ask yourself: why wasn't it written in the past tense?

e) I think the poem does gain by being written in the present tense, because it is easy to imagine a child having written it. If it were in the past tense, the author would be unable to use childlike ideas so effectively, as it would be written from an adult's point of view, i.e. remembering a childhood experience rather than actually carrying it out as is conveyed in the poem. Examples of these childlike ideas are:
'But be careful that your feet aren't sticking out'
'You mustn't sneeze when they come prowling in'.
The present tense allows us actually to feel that the child is desperately hoping that he

is not found, and gives a sense of immediacy and escalation to the poem which would not be conveyed if the poem were in the past tense.

The answer pinpoints the main issues of immediacy and tension, and Kate has referred to specific lines to back up her ideas.

Question f) wanted you to look closely at the last few lines:

f) The writer makes it clear that the others have left the garden by presenting a still, hushed picture of an empty garden into which the child runs when he gives himself up: 'The darkening garden watches. Nothing stirs. The bushes hold their breath; the sun is gone.'
We now have an image of a quiet, deserted garden and can tell that the others have left, obviously having long since tired of searching for their friend. This end to the poem adds an air of mystery to it, which was not present before.

The last question allows you to express your own thoughts. There is no 'right' answer to this question. Everybody feels different things about poems – no two people interpret a poem in exactly the same way. This kind of question allows you to put forward some of your own ideas. This is how Kate interpreted the poem:

g) I think the writer could be trying to do more than describe an experience from childhood, especially from the last line:
'Yes, here you are. But where are they who sought you?'
This could mean that people try to seek your friendship, and once you open up and make yourself vulnerable, i.e. there is no mystery left in the friendship, the interest wanes and they go off to find someone else. Perhaps the writer speaks from past experience, such as a failed relationship that came to an end because it became predictable and mundane. It could also mean that when you think you are wanted, the interest is only superficial and you are wrong, but have made yourself vulnerable anyway.

We'll look at how to tackle Section B in the later sub-section on Using your Imagination.

Plays

Finally, we'll think about the different things that you should be looking for if you get an extract from a play or filmscript for your Understanding section.

As for prose and poetry, you should give your extract three detailed readings, making notes, before you tackle the questions. Keep your eye open for all the techniques we have looked at in the sections on prose and poetry. There are also a number of other things to look out for.

Something to be Seen

First of all, you must try to remember that just as a poem is intended to be read out loud, a play is meant to be *seen* – to be acted on stage. So, when you read an extract from a play your main aim should be to create a picture of what is happening in your mind. You are hoping to respond to the writer's imagination in as full a way as possible.

The relationships and conflicts between characters and the action of a play are presented directly. There is no storyteller to come between the spectator and the writing itself. Therefore, the events taking place on a stage have to speak for themselves. There must be very definite clues by which the spectator can sense what the playwright would like him to think and feel, as there is no narrator to guide him into thinking and feeling a certain way.

This is especially true of the characters. In a play, the writer has quite limited ways of showing you what kind of people he is portraying. He can't tell you what the characters are thinking and feeling, but can only show them speaking and acting. It follows, then, that everything they do and say must tell you something about them, so plays require particularly careful reading. It is very easy just to get wrapped up in what's happening on stage and not to think hard enough about getting to know the characters.

Have a look, for instance, at the following extract, in which two characters, husband and wife, are very clearly depicted:

WILLY: Why don't you open a window in here, for God's sake?

LINDA [*with infinite patience*]: They're all open, dear.

WILLY: The way they boxed us in here. Bricks and windows, windows and bricks.

LINDA: We should've bought the land next door.

WILLY: The street is lined with cars. There's not a breath of fresh air in the neighbourhood. The grass don't grow any more, you can't raise a carrot in the backyard. They should've had a law against apartment houses. Remember those two beautiful elm trees out there? When I and Biff hung the swing between them?

LINDA: Yeah, like being a million miles from the city.

WILLY: They should've arrested the builder for cutting them down. They massacred the neighbourhood. [*Lost*] More and more I think of those days, Linda. This time of year was lilac and wisteria. And then the peonies would come out, and the daffodils. What a fragrance in this room!

LINDA: Well, after all, people had to move somewhere.

WILLY: No, there's more people now.

LINDA: I don't think there's more people, I think –

WILLY: There's more people! That's what's ruining this country! Population is getting out of control. The competition is maddening! Smell the stink from that apartment house! And another one on the other side . . .

(Death of a Salesman by Arthur Miller)*

You can tell from the impatient tone of Willy's voice in the first line that he is frustrated. Everything he says in the passage pushes home the point that he feels imprisoned in the apartment: 'There's not a breath of fresh air in the neighbourhood', 'The way they boxed us in here'. He also thinks longingly of the past: 'More and more I think of those days, Linda', so we get the idea that he must be a bit of a failure, as all he seems to want to do is to look back, and it doesn't sound as if they are living in a very pleasant place. He is also very abrupt with his wife: 'Why don't you open a window in here, for God's sake', and 'There's more people!' In all, he strikes us as a desperately unhappy man, almost driven to nervous collapse by his sense of failure and frustration.

His wife is completely different. She speaks just five lines in the whole extract, and her only desire seems to be to make Willy feel better. She doesn't seem in the least angry with him for snapping at her. When she does try to talk to him properly – perhaps suggesting some disagreement with what he is saying – he cuts her down immediately:

LINDA: Well, after all, people had to move somewhere.

WILLY: No, there's more people now.

LINDA: I don't think there's more people, I think –

WILLY: There's more people!

We understand from the talk of the past that Willy and Linda have been in this place for some time and also that they must have children, by the mention of the swing. Perhaps 'Biff' is one of the children. We also understand that they are living in a town or the suburb of a city. It can't really be the centre of a big city as Willy is continually talking about the time when the street wasn't so crowded.

It is also possible to deduce that Willy has not been very successful financially, as, surely, if he had been able to afford it, they would have moved. The references to the past and the fact that Willy and Linda seem to have no secrets from each other – he speaks to her almost as if she is not there – suggest that they are middle-aged or older.

So, even from a very short extract, we can begin to understand characters, and draw some conclusions about the kind of lives they may have led.

We'll finish the section on Understanding Literary Material with a look at how one student tackled a set of questions on a passage from John Osborne's famous play:

LOOK BACK IN ANGER

JIMMY: You sit there like a lump of dough. I thought you were going to make me some tea.

    [*Cliff groans. Jimmy turns to Alison*]

    Is your friend Webster coming tonight?

ALISON: He might drop in. You know what he is.

JIMMY: Well, I hope he doesn't. I don't think I could take Webster tonight.

ALISON: I thought you said he was the only person who spoke your language.

JIMMY: So he is. Different dialect but same language. I like him. He's got bite, edge, drive –

ALISON: Enthusiasm.

JIMMY: You've got it. When he comes here, I begin to feel exhilarated. He doesn't like me, but he gives me something, which is more than I get from most people. Not since –

ALISON: Yes, we know. Not since you were living with Madeline.

    [*She folds some of the clothes she has already ironed, and crosses to the bed with them.*]

CLIFF: (*behind paper again*). Who's Madeline?

ALISON: Oh, wake up, dear. You've heard about Madeline enough times. She was his mistress. Remember? When he was fourteen. Or was it thirteen?

JIMMY: Eighteen.

ALISON: He owes just about everything to Madeline.

CLIFF: I get mixed up with all your women. Was she the one all those years older than you?

JIMMY: Ten years.

CLIFF: Proper little Marchbanks, you are!

JIMMY: What time's that concert on? (*Checks paper*)

CLIFF: (*yawns*). Oh, I feel so sleepy. Don't feel like standing behind that blinking sweet-stall again tomorrow. Why don't you do it on your own, and let me sleep in?

JIMMY: I've got to be at the factory first thing, to get some more stock, so you'll have to put it up on your own. Another five minutes.

    [*Alison has returned to her ironing board. She stands with her arms folded, smoking, staring thoughtfully*]

    She had more animation in her little finger than you two put together.

CLIFF: Who did?

ALISON: Madeline.

JIMMY: Her curiosity about things, and about people was staggering. It wasn't just a naive nosiness. With her, it was simply the delight of being awake, and watching.

[*Alison starts to press Cliff's trousers*]

CLIFF: (*behind paper*). Perhaps I will make some tea, after all.

JIMMY: (*quietly*). Just to be with her was an adventure. Even to sit on the top of a bus with her was like setting out with Ulysses.

CLIFF: Wouldn't have said Webster was much like Ulysses. He's an ugly little devil.

JIMMY: I'm not talking about Webster, stupid. He's all right, though, in his way. A sort of female Emily Brontë. He's the only one of your friends (*to Alison*) who's worth tuppence, anyway. I'm surprised you get on with him.

ALISON: So is he, I think.

JIMMY: (*rising to window R., and looking out*). He's not only got guts, but sensitivity as well. That's about the rarest combination I can think of. None of your other friends have got either.

ALISON: (*very quietly and earnestly*). Jimmy, please – don't go on.

[*He turns and looks at her. The tired appeal in her voice has pulled him up suddenly. But he soon gathers himself for a new assault. He walks, C., behind Cliff, and stands looking down at his head.*]

JIMMY: Your friends – there's a shower for you.

CLIFF: (*mumbling*). Dry up. Let her get on with my trousers.

JIMMY: (*musingly*). Don't think I could provoke her. Nothing I could do would provoke her. Not even if I were to drop dead.

CLIFF: Then drop dead.

JIMMY: They're either militant like her Mummy and Daddy. Militant, arrogant and full of malice. Or vague. She's somewhere between the two.

CLIFF: Why don't you listen to that concert of yours? And don't stand behind me. That blooming droning on behind me gives me a funny feeling down the spine.

[*Jimmy gives his ears a twist and Cliff roars with pain. Jimmy grins back at him.*]
That hurt, you rotten sadist! (*To Alison*). I wish you'd kick his head in for him.

JIMMY: (*moving in between them*). Have you ever seen her brother? Brother Nigel? The straight-backed, chinless wonder from Sandhurst? I only met him once myself. He asked me to step outside when I told his mother she was evil minded.

LOOK BACK IN ANGER

Questions [Total: 50 marks]

1. What, according to the passage, does Jimmy do for a living?

[2 marks]

2. What kind of person is Jimmy, especially in his attitude to his wife, Alison?

[10 marks]

3. What, as far as we can gather, are the sources of conflict between them?

    [6 marks]

4. What sort of qualities in people does Jimmy admire, and in whom?

    [6 marks]

5. Do you think that there is anything in Alison's or Cliff's behaviour that could be making Jimmy any more angry and frustrated?

    [6 marks]

6. *Either*   Imagine you are Alison, at the end of a Sunday with Jimmy and Cliff. Write a diary extract in which you record the events of the day, and your feelings about your life and about the future.

    or   Imagine you have met Jimmy and Alison for the first time, at a party. In a diary, record your impressions of them, and your feelings about their relationship and about their future.

    [20 marks]

Question 1 simply tested your understanding of the content of the extract:

1. Jimmy works on a sweet-stall, or in a sweet-shop, with Cliff.

Question 2 asked for quite a thorough analysis of Jimmy's behaviour – rather like the analysis required in a similar question on the *Adrian Mole* extract:

2. Jimmy seems very self-centered as all he talks about is himself and other people only in the way they affect him, and his opinions of them. He thinks little of his wife Alison and doesn't show any respect for either her or Cliff. He has the attitude of one who has been hard done by in his life and will never be happy as he constantly compares his present circumstances to a previous happier existence, although one can't help feeling he may be romanticizing his past. He takes out what is a personal lack of contentment on others, especially his wife, and repeatedly refers to his two companions' inadequacies in comparison to his mistress Madeline and Webster, who obviously seem now to have had attributes that he himself lacks, as do Cliff and Alison.

On the surface, Jimmy and Alison seem to have little in common but I think the reason that Jimmy is so disgruntled is that Alison is probably too familiar and he wishes them both to be different: more like Madeline and Webster; so he continues to put her down whilst glorifying others.

At first Jimmy's reference to Madeline in front of his wife seems very cruel and thoughtless but it soon becomes clear that it has been used as a weapon in arguments for a long time.

Jimmy is brutally rude, especially to Alison, insulting her and her family openly. He seems to take a sadistic pleasure in upsetting her.

Aletta not only picks out the relevant details, but shows that she has drawn some conclusions about the underlying reasons for Jimmy's behaviour – his personal discontent.

Question 3 required you to probe more deeply into the source of their misery:

3. The main source of conflict in the passage seems to be Jimmy's sense that everyone around him is tired, boring and lacking in enthusiasm. He feels frustrated and claustrophobic. The situation is made worse when he starts praising Madeline and Webster to Alison, as his constant references to his former girlfriend make her bitter and sarcastic.

Question 4 follows on from 3, testing your awareness of what Jimmy feels his life lacks:

4. Jimmy admires Webster's strong qualities – those often associated with a successful male: sharpness, ambition, energy, sensitivity and 'guts'. In Madeline he admires a sense of wonder and joy, and her interest in all that is going on around her. In both people, he seems to admire those qualities absent from the people he now lives with.

Here, you had to isolate the relevant points in the extract, and to relate Jimmy's admiration of others to his own life.

You have looked at Jimmy: now you are asked to look at Cliff and Alison:

5. Cliff's apparent laziness could be contributing to Jimmy's anger. He also seems to side with Alison against her husband when he says things like 'I wish you'd kick his head in for him'. He has a tendency to provoke Jimmy and make Alison feel even more bitter, in lines such as 'I get mixed up with all your women'. He generally does nothing to make things smoother between husband and wife.

Alison's continued sarcasm, and her goading of Jimmy, are worse than silence. She irritates him with her continual reminders that 'she has heard it all before', such as 'I thought you said he was the only person who spoke your language', and 'He owes just about everything to Madeline'. Her calmness and inertia seem to aggravate Jimmy – he cannot get any response from her, even of anger.

Aletta has poinpointed the difficulties, here, and has shown sensitivity to this tense three-cornered relationship.

We'll look at how to answer Question 6 in the next sub-section on Using your Imagination.

Using your Imagination

If you are taking an examination, you will find that in the section of the paper which requires you to answer questions on literary material there will always be one question asking you to do something rather unusual, such as, 'Imagine you are the girl in this poem. Write a diary extract describing what happens to you.'

These questions ask you to enter imaginatively into the feelings of characters in the passages, or perhaps to imagine a similar situation and write about it, or even to write about what might happen next. You not only need to understand what you have read very thoroughly, you also need to demonstrate your own expressive skills once again.

You must remember that this is not strictly speaking 'expressive writing'. You will generally find that what you are being asked to do is transform ideas, information, feelings conveyed in the extracts into another form. You will be using details from the original passage or poem to write your answer which will be very closely related to the original – a kind of joint effort between the writer's imagination and your own.

It is all too easy to get carried away, writing your own creative piece and forgetting completely about the original. You will get no marks for a good or even excellent piece of writing which has nothing to do with the passage or poem it is based on. The examiners will be looking to see how successfully you have used your 'stimulus' material. They are not just interested in how well you can write.

Earlier on, we examined three possible GCSE question papers on prose, a poem and a play extract. We'll now look at how some students (not always the same ones) got on with those 'imaginative' questions which appeared at the end.

First of all, let's turn back to the two extracts about old people. The question was:

'Imagine that you are an elderly person reading these two passages. Give your impression of the two young people involved.'

Before you start to write, there are several things you need to do:

1. Underline all the relevant information: that is, the details about both characters' behaviour.
2. Make notes as to what each detail tells us about them.
3. Make notes on how these behavioural details might seem to a much older person. Is there anything they might misinterpret?

4. Put the points to be made in the order that you think they would strike an older person.

Once you have made these notes, you can weave them into a coherent piece of writing – but there is something else to consider, and this is where your imagination comes in. The question asks you quite clearly to imagine that you are an elderly person. Obviously, the examiners want you to get over some of the flavour of the personality and the way of thinking of an elderly person. So, you are not only conveying your understanding of the passage, but also showing how well you can create a character – that of the elderly person you are becoming as you write your answer.

The same rules apply to question 4, where you are asked to write a diary extract including 'the important things that [Marian] notices and what she feels about them'. You also need to get over a strong sense of Marian's personality.

This is how Lola tackled the question: 'Imagine that Marian keeps a diary. Write her diary entry for the day she visits the Home. Include the important things that she notices and what she feels about them. Bear in mind that a diary entry need not be too long (see Adrian Mole's).'

Dear Diary,
I had such an awful day! I mentioned before that today I was going to an old ladies' Home because doing things like that earns you lots of points for campfire. Well, when I found out what the Home was like I wouldn't have made the effort to get those points at all. First of all, there was this frightening sort of nurse, who could have been a man in disguise and was really unfriendly. The Home itself looked like a prison because it had all these closed doors with the women inside. I really didn't want to go in any of them and discover what kind of horrors lay inside. The whole place was cold and unfriendly.
   I thought that I would be able to hear the old ladies chatting and that they would be walking around as they pleased, but there was absolutely no noise and it seemed as if they were confined to their rooms.
   The floor outside the rooms felt springy and strange, and when I followed the nurse on it I heard what sounded like a sheep bleating inside one of the rooms. This was really beginning to frighten me when the door of this room started to open gradually with an old woman grinning behind it like a witch. I would have run away if the nurse hadn't pushed me in. The room was very dark and wet, crowded with ugly, damp furniture. There was another skeleton lying on the bed – she might have been dead because she didn't move at all. The first old lady took my cap – I don't know why – and I just stood there, in their dungeon, terrified.
   What a nightmare!

You can see that Lola keeps to a fairly simple vocabulary and makes sure that it sounds as if a young girl is writing this diary. She has not put any of her own feelings – of pity for the inmates, for instance – into the answer, but has stuck very closely to what she has been given in the original. This is the real key to writing successful answers to such questions – you need to learn just how much you can use your own imagination, and stop before you get too carried away.

We'll turn again, now, to 'Hide and Seek' (p. 79). The last question in this section was:

'Imagine you are the person in the poem, and that you have found your friends again. Describe what happens, how you behave and what is said. (You may write in playscript, poetry or prose.)'

Kate chose to write a poem:

> *The trees stare, silently reproachful.*
> *I leave the garden,*
> *Sadly trailing my knitted coat behind me.*
> *My mouth droops and eyelids are pricking*
> *Where have they gone?*
> *The cold of the toolshed floor still*
> *Lies like wet fish on my legs.*
> *The dusty, grainy smell lingers.*
> *Knees dirty*
> *Hands ashen from time spent in old sacks*
> *Eyes accustomed tô the pale sky –*
> *Gently fading but lighter than toolsheds.*
> *Where have they gone?*
> *I find no answer in the whispering bushes*
> *And silent reeds.*
> *Childish nose stings with indignant snot*
> *Eyes fat with ready tears.*
> *'Where have you been, Jack, mother's angry'*
> *I spin round, stupidly.*
> *They are here.*
> *Sister with hands on hips*
> *A child's mocking parody of maternal authority.*
> *'We looked for you for hours, didn't you hear us calling?'*
> *'No.'*

Sister thins her lips into a tight pink line.
'Mother's angry with you, says you always have to make things difficult.'
I ignore it, knowing that I am expected to react with virulence.
'Where were you anyway?'
Shadow of agitation passes over me.
'Not telling.'
'Oh, go on.'
'No.'
'See if I care. Who wants to know where you were hiding anyway.'
I feel better but hurt that I was so readily deserted.
'Bet he was behind the barrow in the orchard.'
'Was not.'
I know something you don't know.
Brother kicks an apple rife with fruit flies.
'Mother says you're to have no dinner.'
I remain silent.
Was it my fault they couldn't find me?
An unfair punishment but see if I care.
Just see if I care.
I can use that hiding place again.
And no one can seek me out.
We can have a secret gang in the toolshed
Where no one will find us.
Pirates and cowboy games will be
Filled with a mysterious excitement.
I am still not ready to forgive
But have almost already forgotten.

Notice how she has picked out details from the original poem which help to make the two poems into a whole. She begins with the garden, and refers to the salty toolshed smell in her first few lines. She conveys the sense of mystery we felt at the end of 'Hide and Seek' in the lines 'I heard no answer in the whispering bushes/And silent reeds'. She also gets over the strong sense of injustice and anger felt by the child. The sister is an excellent creation – her behaviour quite in keeping with the atmosphere of the original poem.

This piece of writing is unmistakably Kate's own, yet is so clearly based on the original, using so many of its details and feelings, that both requirements of the question are fulfilled: that of understanding and of writing expressively.

Finally, we'll turn to *Look Back in Anger* again. The last question on this paper was:

'Imagine you have met Jimmy and Alison for the first time, at a party. In a diary, record your impressions of them, and your feelings about their relationship and about their future.'

There are two students' answers here. Both of them use similar details and information from the original, yet their answers are very different, although equally successful, because in their writing they have each created quite distinct personalities. Again, we can see the combination of understanding and expressive writing at its most successful:

Nisha

Went to Isabella's party with Ronnie. It would have been fine if not for a couple that seemed to latch on to me at the buffet table. As far as I could gather their names were Jimmy and Alison. I couldn't really get a word in edgeways. That man Jimmy was rambling on and on and in such superior tones! Poor old Alison looked fed up to the back teeth with the whole set-up (party, people, Jimmy in particular and life in general).

In my opinion Jimmy seemed to take everything for granted, especially Alison. He seemed to think that he had the right to walk all over people verbally and that he was all-important. God, that sort of person annoys me so much. When I spoke to Isabella briefly at the end of the party she said that she thought the only reason he went on like that was because he didn't think he was as good as anyone else, inside. The only reason that they came apparently was because her father was something rather important in the army and Alison's brother was in the same regiment and very good friends with Isabella's brother at Sandhurst. Nigel unfortunately couldn't make it to the party. I rather like him, at least he has a sense of honour and duty, unlike some, namely Jimmy.

I personally found them both rather annoying. Alison, I think, might have had something to say had she been given a chance to say it but otherwise she did not say or do anything much at all apart from smoke, look sullen, eat and drink, grimace when Jimmy said anything embarrassing or stupid (which was quite often) and look around at other people in groups having a good time.

At one point I tried to escape by visiting the loo to 'powder my nose' but when I emerged I found them both waiting just by the door to grab me as I came out and drag me into conversation again. I didn't have the heart to disappear after that as I felt certain that Jimmy would have said something nasty to Alison had I gone. I wasn't really concentrating on what he was saying properly but I did manage to hear something about a mistress – Madeline or Marilyn – why on earth drag her into the conversation?

Another thing that he said several times was that nobody would care if he fell down dead. I could not have agreed more with him but had to make the right, sympathetic noises. I think he only said it to attract attention and sympathy. When Alison heard him say this she did not utter a word or even look surprised or shocked but merely went on smoking. I think she probably felt there was no point speaking to him.

It's really sad to see a couple like that who no longer suit each other or get on. I think they are so fed up they can't be bothered any more. I don't expect they'll last very much longer unless Jimmy changes. If this is the best they can do together, they'd probably be better off apart.

Aletta

This afternoon I went to a party and unfortunately got stuck on a sofa in between a couple: Jimmy and Alison, neighbours of my host. Usually I manage to extricate myself from such situations, but I felt rather sorry for them, so endured their conversation for a whole two hours! At first I thought it might be quite interesting as Jimmy, a rather handsome man, showed a great interest in my recent holiday to France and took great pleasure in my descriptions of the coastline and various sights.

Alison stayed quiet at first, remaining unsmiling on my left. Then gradually she began to say more, but only in the form of 'little digs' and sarcastic remarks aimed at her husband. Soon Jimmy's conversation turned into more of a subtle attack on his wife though he still channelled it through his conversation with me. I began to feel uncomfortable as their feelings, or in fact their lack of feeling for each other, came through. Jimmy soon turned out to be the more vicious of the two and anything Alison said to me he tore to shreds in such a callous way, it left me quite shocked. Perhaps the oddest thing was that Alison did little to defend herself.

I began to wonder why on earth they had married but there was something that seemed to hold them together, though it was admittedly a very weak bond – or so it seemed. I couldn't help feeling that if they carried on like this they would drive each other mad: they nearly did it to me. I really felt that they needed, what is so tactfully called these days, professional help.

Those of you doing 100 per cent coursework will also have to write in timed conditions, using literary material as a stimulus, and you should make sure that you, too, get plenty of practice.

Some of you will find this part of the course very straightforward; others will find that this kind of semi-expressive writing takes you some time to master. Don't worry – be persistent, and you will find that it gradually gets easier and easier. Remember, the more you read, the more capable you will find yourself of dealing with all different kinds of literary material.

UNDERSTANDING PERSUASIVE, INFORMATIVE AND ARGUMENTATIVE WRITING

The GCSE examiners are very concerned that you should be able to spot the difference between *facts* and *ideas and opinions* when you are writing and reading. We have already said that facts can be used imaginatively. You may be asked to examine the kind of writing in which facts are used in this way on your course or in the Understanding section of your examination.

Sometimes it is quite difficult to draw a dividing line between facts and opinions. *Facts* are things which no one can dispute, like the sun rising in the east and setting in the west, and that zebras are black and white. *Opinions* are often (though not always) based on facts. For instance, if someone said to you that because there is so much suffering in the world, God can't exist, they would be expressing an opinion. However, this opinion would be based on a fact: no one can deny that there is suffering in the world, but you could easily argue with the conclusion that God does not exist.

There are also *ideas*, and these may have no factual basis at all. Someone might have an idea that Shakespeare was actually a woman, but he'd have trouble backing his idea up! However, when Einstein had an idea about relativity it *was* backed up by facts, and by opinions drawn from facts. So, you need to be very careful in sorting out facts, opinions, and ideas, as you read through any non-literary piece of writing.

To help you to learn how to do so, we'll have a look at two passages from the same book, the first of which is entirely factual:

The canopy itself, the ceiling of the jungle, is a dense continuous layer of greenery some 6 or 7 metres deep. Each leaf in it is accurately angled to ensure that it will collect the maximum amount of light. Many have a special joint at the base of the stalk that enables them to twist and follow the sun as it swings overhead from east to west each day. All except the topmost layer are largely screened from the wind, so the air around them is warm and humid.

This description of a rain-forest canopy has been written simply to inform, and is packed with scientifically sound facts. There are no descriptive words designed to get an emotional response from the reader. The only adjectives are factual ones, such as 'continuous', 'warm', 'humid'.

But later in the book, the author uses the powerful armour of facts he has built up about the rain forest to launch a deeply felt plea against the destruction of the planet. His facts become the basis for his argument, and our awareness of these facts makes it very difficult for us to disagree with him:

The other great natural resource of the world, second only to the oceans, is the tropical rain forest. That too is being plundered in a similarly reckless way. We know that it plays a key role in the worldwide balance of life, absorbing the heavy equatorial rains and releasing them in a steady flow down the rivers to irrigate the lower fertile valley. It has given us immense riches. Some 40 per cent of all the drugs we use contain natural ingredients, many of them deriving from the forest. Timber from the trunks of its trees is the most valued of all wood. For centuries, foresters have collected it, seeking particular kinds of trees, pulling them out and leaving the rest of the forest community little damaged. They planned their activities carefully so that they did not return to the same area for several years and gave the forest time to recover.

But now pressures on the rain forest have intensified. The increase of human beings in the surrounding countryside has led, understandably, to more and more of the jungle being cut down so that the land can be used to grow food. As we now know, the fertility of the jungle lies more in the substance of its plants than in its leached-out soil and the cleared land becomes exhausted and infertile after a few years. So the people fell more forest. Adding to this encroachment, modern machinery makes it easier than ever before to turn timber into cash. A tree that took two centuries to grow can now be knocked down in an hour. Powerful tractors can drag the fallen trees out through dense forest with comparative ease, even if, in the process, they destroy many other trees that have no immediate cash value. So the jungle is disappearing at a swifter rate than ever before. Every year an area the size of Switzerland is being cut down. Once it has gone, the roots of the trees no longer hold the soil together. The lashing rains wash it away. So the rivers turn to brown roaring torrents, the land becomes a soil-less waste and the richest treasury of plants and animals in the world has vanished.

The roll call of such ecological disasters could be extended almost endlessly. It is only too easy to demonstrate the damage we have now inflicted on the wildernesses of the world. It is more important to consider what should be done about it.

(The Living Planet by David Attenborough)

What a different piece of writing this second extract is. Look at how the author hits us with facts so that we accept his use of emotionally charged words to describe how the rain forest is being used. For instance, he begins by saying that the rain forest is being 'plundered in a . . . reckless way' – which certainly arouses our indignation. Then he follows this comment up with a whole list of facts about its role in the balance of life, and its importance as a source of timber and drugs. In the second paragraph, he again turns facts into emotionally charged statements such as 'A tree that took two centuries to grow can now be knocked down in an hour' and 'Every year an area the size of

Switzerland is being cut down'. Words and phrases guaranteed to play on our feelings are continually used: 'soil-less waste', 'richest treasury', 'ecological disasters', 'damage'. It is a very effective piece of writing indeed – and its effectiveness comes through the use of facts as a rock-solid basis for heartfelt opinions.

The next extract is also intended to persuade us over to a certain point of view, but the technique is totally different. It is a review of a party political broadcast on TV and here, certain 'facts' are used in a highly amusing way to make us laugh and surely to feel that the programme was every bit as funny as Clive James says it was:

The worst TV programme of this or any other week was the Conservative Party Political Broadcast (all channels) which twice referred to a Russian writer called Solzhenitskyn.

If Solzhenitskyn is against socialism, we should be too: that was the message. The message was somewhat weakened by the fact that there is no such writer as Solzhenitskyn. The man they mean is called Solzhenitsyn – there is a 'ts' but there is no 'k'. The pronunciation 'Solzhenitskyn' was invented last year by Margaret Thatcher, who thereby suggested that she knew nothing about Solzhenitsyn's writings beyond what she had heard from her advisers, who in turn had apparently mixed him up with Rumpelstiltskin.

Other attractions of the Tory PPB included Reg Prentice, who was to be seen sitting in the path of a Force 10 gale, apparently in order to demonstrate that sparse, lank hair looks very ratty in a high wind. Possessing even less hair than Reg, I can advise him that the thing to do is cut it short. Growing it long and winding it round your head like a coil of rope is effective only if you fix the result with Araldite and wear a motor-cycle helmet when out of doors. Lectures on personal freedom lose force when delivered by someone who looks in desperate need of Supplementary Benefit.

(*The Crystal Bucket*: TV criticism from *The Observer* 1976–79 by Clive James)

Note that Clive James says nothing whatsoever about the political points made in the broadcast. Like a caricaturist, he picks the most amusing moments, blows them up, and manages to make the whole thing seem ridiculous. It is an excellent example of how material can be slanted to make people think certain things. David Attenborough uses facts, Clive James uses his gift for comedy.

Sometimes, a writer can almost fool a reader into thinking he is reading facts when he is actually being given a writer's opinions. In an article called 'The Sporting Spirit', George Orwell makes use of a recent event to express his opinion on sport. In 1945, Moscow Dynamos, a Russian football team, toured Britain, playing against leading British football clubs. There was some ill feeling between the two sides, and Orwell uses this *fact* as a basis for his opinions, expressed in this paragraph:

Now that the brief visit of the Dynamo football team has come to an end, it is possible to say publicly what many thinking people were saying privately before the Dynamos ever arrived. That is, that sport is an unfailing cause of ill-will, and that if such a visit as this had any effect at all on Anglo-Soviet relations, it could only be to make them slightly worse than before.

('The Sporting Spirit' by George Orwell)

Now, you could be forgiven for feeling that the second sentence has been made to sound more like a fact than an opinion and it is clearly Orwell's intention that it should come over to us with the same impact that a fact would have. He goes on to give details of some of the events which fuel his opinion, constantly manipulating facts towards one end. It is very difficult indeed to keep yourself conscious of the reality.

If you were arguing the opposite point of view to Orwell's, you could say that the conflict between the teams was just bad luck. You would choose completely different, but equally effective, examples to support *your* arguments. If you used your material as well as Orwell uses his, you could write an equally powerful essay in support of sport as a unifying force in society. Facts can be used for many purposes!

UNDERSTANDING FACTUAL, DIAGRAMMATIC AND PICTORIAL INFORMATION

Language does not always come in the form of prose and poetry. Remember that whenever we try to make sense of a bus timetable or read an advertisement, we are using our understanding of 'English'. You also need to have a sound grasp of the language to do well in all your other subjects at school – otherwise you will find yourself unable to read a map or a graph successfully. The GCSE examiners have recognized how vital English is for many of the activities and careers you may be pursuing in the future, as well as for your other subjects, and have made understanding this kind of material an essential part of the course.

So during your course, and perhaps in the examination itself, you may be

BBC External Services

LONDON CALLING...
732 hours 45 mins
in 37 languages

Czech/Slovak
Polish
Hungarian
Finnish

Romanian
Bulgarian
Serbo-Croat
Slovene

Portuguese (also for Brazil)
Greek
Turkish

Central European
Service
72:45

German Service
22:45

Russian Service
46:00

South East European
Service
42:30

South European
Service
41:15

French Service
35:00

For Europe
For Africa

African Service
22:45

Latin American Service
31:30

Far Eastern Service
50:30

Eastern Service
60:30

Arabic Service
63:00

English
by Radio
41:30

Spanish
Hausa/Somali/Swahili

Mandarin
Cantonese
Indonesian
Vietnamese
Japanese
Thai
Malay

Hindi
Persian
Urdu
Bengali
Burmese
Pashto
Tamil
Nepali

required to look at charts, maps, advertisements, statistics, timetables, graphs, tables, diagrams, photographs and plans, and to answer questions on them. As with literary, non-literary and journalistic material, you can work out a logical, methodical approach to the understanding of this kind of material which will help you to obtain the maximum amount of information from it.

There are many different diagrammatic ways in which information may be presented, and of which you will need to make sense. We'll have a look at some of the most common.

Pie Charts

They usually look like the one opposite – although this one is rather glamorous:

This chart is designed to show how much radio broadcasting time is devoted to each language on the BBC World Service. Pie charts are usually used to show how much time and/or money is going into something. The kind of question you might be asked on them would be: 'Which is the most frequently heard language other than English in the BBC external services?' (the answer is Arabic) or, 'On which service would you hear the greatest variety of languages?' (Eastern, with eight languages). This type of question would test your basic understanding. You might also be asked to write a report summarizing the information given in the chart (for a method of approaching diagrammatic material, see p. 103 and for a worked example, pp. 104–108).

Bar Charts

These are generally used to draw comparisons, as in the following chart:

Here, we can see how the BBC compares with all its competitors in its external output.

Questions on such a chart might include: 'Which country is Britain's greatest rival in airtime?' (USA), or 'Which language is heard most frequently on international airwaves?' (English, in the USA, UK and Indian external services). Again, you might be asked to write a report summarizing the statistics. You may also be required to use information in a report from both bar and pie charts.

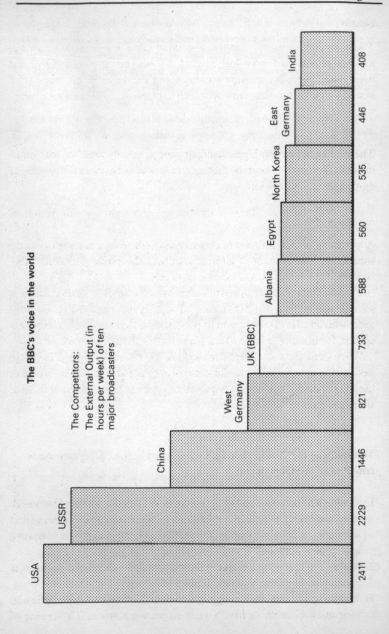

The BBC's voice in the world

The Competitors:
The External Output (in hours per week) of ten major broadcasters

USA 2411
USSR 2229
China 1446
West Germany 821
UK (BBC) 733
Albania 588
Egypt 560
North Korea 535
East Germany 446
India 408

Graphs

These usually measure changes. For instance, a graph might chart the number of hours an individual watches TV between the ages of five and twenty-five. It would measure increases and decreases in the number of hours. You would use the same approach to graphs as to bar and pie charts.

Maps

These often appear on Understanding papers, usually together with other material. You need to examine them carefully, and not to make the mistake of thinking they are irrelevant.

Advertisements

Advertisements are designed to persuade you – the consumer – to buy or do something. The amount of information about the product or commodity contained in advertisements varies enormously.

You will certainly be required to look at different kinds of advertisement at some stage in your GCSE course. You may be required to say how successful an advertisement is in its persuasive techniques, or to compare it against, for instance, a letter of complaint stating the reality of the product.

When examining an advertisement, look for: use of word-play; language designed to appeal to the emotions; use of graphics and colour; information used to persuade. You may be required to comment on one or all of these in an examination or on your course.

Techniques for Answering Questions on Factual, Diagrammatic and Pictorial Information

1. Decide why the diagram has been drawn. What is its purpose? What does it tell you? Is it illustrating comparisons between things? Or showing that something is increasing or decreasing? What is the map of? Does it serve any specific purpose?
2. Make sure that you understand the general drift of the information it is giving you. Don't worry about details, yet.
3. Write a brief sentence in rough summarizing this general drift, to fix it in your mind. Something like, 'Graph measuring hours of TV viewing of

11–18 year olds, year by year. Shows that viewing increases dramatically during 12th–14th years' would do fine.

4. Go on to the questions. Take each separately. For each one, comb the diagram and/or other material for relevant information and note it down in rough.

5. Rearrange the information to present a logical answer. Discard anything that is not relevant. Do not add any of your own details.

6. Leave five minutes at the end to check that you have written clear, fluent, accurate English. Don't forget spelling and punctuation.

Let's have a brief look at the kind of material you may be asked to read, understand and then use to answer questions. This analysis of the output of Channel 4 and ITV can be used in a number of ways. There are basic questions that can be asked (1–3), there is a summary to write (4) and we can put forward opinions about the kind of viewers watching Channel 4 and ITV based on the information (5–6).

PROGRAMME TRANSMISSIONS ON CHANNEL 4

(Weekly Average, Year Ended 30th March 1986)

	DURATION Hrs.Mins.	PERCENTAGE %
News	4:02	5½
Current affairs and general factual	14:18	19
Arts	2:17	3
Religion	1:39	2¼
Education	7:56	10½
INFORMATIVE	30:12	40¼
Plays, series, TV movies	16:05	21½
Feature films	11:45	15½
NARRATIVE	27:50	37
Entertainment and light music	11:00	14½
Sport	6:07	8¼
TOTAL ALL PROGRAMMES	75:16††	100

††Opening captions totalling 7 minutes per week are not specified above but are included in the total.

(IBA Yearbook 1987 'Television and Radio 1987')

PROGRAMME TRANSMISSIONS ON ITV*		

(*Weekly Average, Year Ended* 30*th March* 1986)

	DURATION Hrs./Mins.	PERCENTAGE %
News and news magazines	11:01	10½
Current affairs and general factual	10:54	10¼
Arts	0:42	¾
Religion	2:31	2½
Adult education	1:51†	1¾
School programmes	6:50	6½
Pre-school	3:35	3½
Children's informative programmes	2:12	2
INFORMATIVE	39:36	37¾
Plays, series, TV movies	26:21	25
Feature films	8:18	8
NARRATIVE	34:39	33
Children's drama and entertainment	7:24	7
Entertainment and light music	14:29	13¾
Sport	9:00	8½
TOTAL ALL PROGRAMMES	105:15††	100

Excluding TV-am's 21 hours per week.

†*To this total should be added* 13 *minutes per week of general factual material shown at peak time which was accepted by the* IBA *as educationally valuable and supported by educational material and activities.*

††*Opening captions totalling 7 minutes per week are not specified above, but are included in the total.*

The first three questions might be on the content of the table, to make sure you had understood:

1. Which type of programme receives the least airtime on ITV? Which is given the most?

Answer: Arts programmes receive the least airtime on ITV, and plays, series and TV movies are given the most.

You would arrive at this answer by first of all looking at the right-hand table. You will see that the Duration column tells you how much time per week is devoted to different types of programme. Types of programme are divided into 'informative' and 'narrative'. If you run your eye down the column it is easy to see that the smallest figure is 0.42 for arts, and 26.21 the largest, for plays, series, TV movies. You would need to be careful not to make the mistake of thinking that 'informative' was a specific type of programme, rather than general. You would need to work out that these were more inclusive categories.

2. Which type of programme receives the least airtime on Channel 4, and which the most?

Answer: Religious programmes receive the least airtime on Channel 4, and plays, series, TV movies the most.

The same principles as for question 1 apply, but of course you use the left-hand table.

3. How do Channel 4 and ITV compare in the number of hours of viewing time available to them?

Answer: ITV have more viewing hours available to them: a total of 105.15. Channel 4 have a total of 75.16 available to them.

You would arrive at this answer by looking at the totals at the bottom of the left-hand columns of both tables.

The next question might ask you to provide a summary of some or all of these statistics – a 'report'. To do this, you would put the information into a piece of condensed continuous prose. In a *report*, you need to make your sentences as short and compact as possible. Your writing must be clear, precise and logical. You must not include any information not given to you. Use as few adjectives as possible, and don't try to appeal to your readers' emotions.

4. Write a short report summarizing the information on percentage figures provided by the two tables.

Answer: In the average week, about 37 per cent of ITV's total transmissions were informative, 33 per cent narrative, 22 per cent entertainment, light music and sport, and 7 per cent children's drama and entertainment. On Channel 4, a slightly higher percentage of approximately 40 per cent of programmes were informative, 37 per cent narrative, 14 per cent entertainment and music, 8 per cent sport. Channel 4 devoted more airtime to informative and narrative programmes and slightly less to programmes designed mainly to entertain. Both channels had a similar sport output.

You would arrive at this answer in four stages:

i. Make notes in rough of all the relevant information: in this case the percentage figures from both tables.

ii. Decide on the best order in which to present this information. In this case, it seemed sensible to summarize the information on ITV first, then turn to Channel 4, including comparisons where they were relevant.

iii. Write a rough draft of your report, making it as clear and logical as possible.

iv. Write your report out neatly, checking as you do so for spelling mistakes, accuracy and fluency.

The final questions might ask you to draw conclusions about the different kinds of people watching Channel 4 and ITV:

5. From the information given here, is it possible to say whether or not these TV companies are aiming their programmes at different audiences? Give evidence for your answer. If so, in what ways might the viewers differ in their expectations and requirements from TV?

Answer: ITV provide a very high output of programmes of mainly 'entertainment' value: a total of 62 per cent of their total transmission, if sport is included as entertainment. This would suggest that viewers who tune in to ITV would be looking primarily for entertainment and relaxation rather than for programmes of mainly educational value. The large percentage of 'entertainment' programmes suggests that ITV are meeting this demand for 'relaxing' rather than 'educative' viewing, perhaps after a hard day's work. There is, however, a high percentage of news and current affairs programmes (22.75 per cent) so viewers clearly do expect to be kept up to date as well as being entertained.

Children would be much more likely to watch ITV as 7.2 hours a week are devoted to children's TV, as opposed to nothing on Channel 4. There are also a number of school, pre-school and children's informative programmes (13.75 per cent of the total output).

Channel 4 provide a correspondingly high percentage of 'entertainment' programmes (59.75 per cent), so again the implication is that Channel 4 viewers also expect more than anything else to be entertained when they switch on the television. However, the total percentage of viewing time devoted to current affairs, arts, religious and adult educational programmes is much higher than that of ITV. People interested in these areas would be likely to watch Channel 4 more often than ITV.

Some analysis of the range of films and plays shown on both channels would make comment on the possible viewing public of both channels more accurate.

To arrive at this answer, you would need to make a much closer comparison of the two tables. You would look at total percentages of entertainment and informative programmes to see where the differences lay, and draw conclusions on the viewer's expectations from those differences.

Again, your method would be that given for number 4. Note that in this question you are being asked to draw conclusions and give opinions, not simply to produce facts in a different form.

The next possible question moves you even further away from the facts, but you must still remember that *answers are only relevant if based on the information provided.* Such questions as these are an open invitation to irrelevant waffle, so be warned:

6. Imagine you have to write a short description (no more than 100 words) of the kind of viewer at whom Channel 4 *or* ITV are aiming their programmes. You are doing this for an advertising company who are preparing a campaign for one of the companies. Write in full sentences and include details of the lifestyle, type of house, profession or job, and hobbies of the viewer.

Answer: *Target viewer for Channel 4*

Mr X lives in Edgbaston, near Birmingham, in a three-bedroomed detached house, and works as a marketing manager for a publishing company in central Birmingham. Because of his job, he needs to keep up with financial affairs in the city and also with the arts and media worlds generally. His interests include travel and the arts and he always visits concerts or a play when he goes to London. He enjoys watching films to relax after a busy day and likes rugby and golf. He is married, with no children.

This question is not too difficult if you have been accurate and detailed in your answer to question 5. You would need to go through the following steps to answer it adequately:

i. Make rough notes on the information you intend to use (i.e. increased arts output, high percentage of films, high current affairs output).

ii. Try to 'see' the sort of person who would benefit from what Channel 4 provide, and make brief notes on him or her.

iii. Write up your profile in clear and logical English.

Your answer would need to be imaginative but very firmly based on the information provided. There would be no room for humour or sarcasm. You would need to check your rough draft to ensure you had not gone over the word limit.

Finally, here's an example of how a student answered a paper requiring her to make sense of two maps as well as some factual written information, to select relevant details, and then to transform them into a letter and a newspaper report.

Look carefully at Map A which shows you the start and Map B which shows the route of the London Marathon. Then read the passage which follows them. When you have

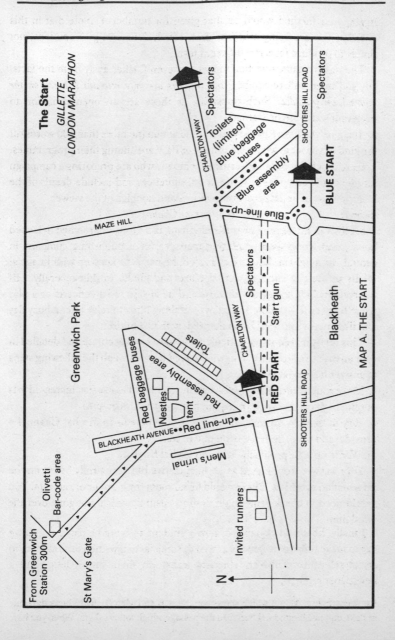

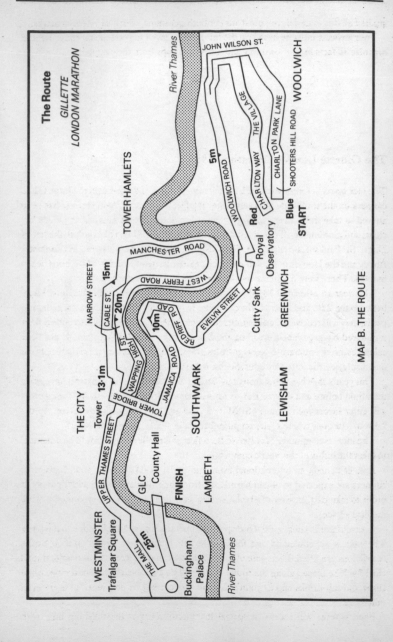

studied all this material, you must answer both questions, which carry equal marks.

Your answers must be based on the information given to you but you must use and organize all facts in your own way and not simply copy from the passage.

The Gillette London Marathon 1983

The race starts in Greenwich Park at 9.30 a.m., 8 April, and finishes at the large GLC car park on the south side of Westminster Bridge. This year's 26-mile route has been altered to take the runners through central London and past many of the city's key sights and monuments. These include the *Cutty Sark*, the Tower of London, the Isle of Dogs, St Paul's Cathedral, Trafalgar Square, Buckingham Palace, Westminster Abbey and the Houses of Parliament. The present series of London Marathons began in 1981. There were 6,700 starters and the race ended in a dead heat.

This year an estimated 18,000 runners will have registered at the Piccadilly Hotel between the 24th and 27th of March where, in return for their numbered registration cards, they will receive official numbered running bibs. Here they will also collect their numbered baggage labels enabling them to deposit their clothing, though not their valuables, on the numerous baggage buses provided. The appropriate bus is simply the one displaying the initial letter of the runner's surname.

This year's race has two starting positions. The blue start is for men who have run a marathon before and the red start is for women and 'first time' men. All competitors will enter Greenwich Park by St Mary's Gate and will report, ready to run, to the Olivetti Marquee where their computer bar codes will be speedily checked.

The increased number of coffee stalls, toilets and rubbish skips should be adequate to meet the influx of this year's competitors.

It is, of course, an international event run under WCCA rules, and all overseas runners are expected to obtain permission from their own governing athletic body in order to take part. In view of previous years' casualties, all runners are urged to seek medical advice.

To avoid traffic jams, special transport will operate from central London to the Park. The race is scheduled to last four and a half hours, after which time all traffic restrictions are lifted. Each mile of the race is indicated by signposts and large digital clocks will be placed along the route. Water will be available at every odd mile, while sugar and salt drinks and St John's first aid services will be positioned at every even mile.

Each entrant will receive a special marathon medal at the finishing line, with chocolate buns, Bovril and fruit drinks made available by courtesy of the G L C. The official awards ceremony will take place at the Inigo Jones Church in the evening and this is followed by a party in Covent Garden Market. The official results will be published in *Running* magazine.

1 Write a letter from the Race Director to this year's entrants, selecting from the passage whatever information you find appropriate. Begin your letter 'Dear Competitor', and end with 'Yours sincerely', followed by your signature. Before starting read the following information carefully.

   It is mid March, which is the date when the Race Director, Mr Ron Fitt, has to contact all the runners taking part in the Gillette London Marathon, 1983, in order to give them all the information they will require together with some helpful advice. His fellow organizers are anxious to avoid two particular problems which existed last year and have urged him to mention the following matters:

   i)   The organizers had received a number of complaints about the amount of litter left in Greenwich Park.
   ii) The unruly behaviour of a minority of competitors at the starting line had caused a slight delay to the race.

   Although Mr Fitt is anxious to emphasize such concerns, he does wish to make the letter suitably encouraging and welcoming.

                                                                              (30 marks)

2 Write a newspaper article using the following information.

   One of the competitors in the London Marathon was a local teacher, Peter Blake, who ran to raise money for a local charity. Details of the organization and its requirements are given in the reporter's notes below.

   Imagine that you are a reporter on a local, weekly paper. You have interviewed Mr Blake and the warden, Mrs Morgan. Selecting what you consider to be suitable information from the maps, the passage and your notes write an article to appear in next week's edition. The article must be of general interest and have a headline. Subheadings may also be used.

   The following is an extract from your reporter's notebook.
   London Marathon – see maps and articles in office for background information.
   Runner – Peter Blake, aged 30; local teacher.
   Charity – PHAB (Physically Handicapped Able Bodied). A local organization.
   Warden – Mrs Morgan
   Problem – centre needs new reception area; aim – handicapped to man reception area i.e.

new telephone (push button, at wheelchair height)
typewriter (electric for light touch)
dictaphone (foot pedal and elbow switch for easy use)
Mrs Morgan said, 'This will enable the handicapped people here to do a real job and save us money.'

(*30 marks*)

(Southern Examining Group GCSE English Syllabus A
Specimen Paper 1988)

You should always read the instructions at the beginning of the examination paper very carefully, as they give you very exact information about how you should answer. The rubric for this paper is very helpful:

Look carefully at Map A, which shows you the start, and Map B, which shows the route of the London Marathon. Then read the passage which follows them. When you have studied all this material, you must answer both questions, which carry equal marks.

Your answers must be based on the information given to you but *you must use and organize all facts in your own way and not simply copy from the passage.*

The words which I have italicized indicate how important that rearrangement of information we have mentioned before really is. Also, note that they stress the need to use your own words.

Approaching this paper, you would first go through these stages:

1. Examine both maps closely.
2. Read through the factual material twice, to familiarize yourself with it.

Question 1's rubric is very thorough. You are given information on how to begin and end the letter, you are told the date, who the letter is from and who will be receiving it, and the two areas it is to cover. You are also given guidance on its tone: encouraging and welcoming as well as expressing concern.

Before you wrote your first draft, you would go through your factual material, underlining and making a note of each piece of relevant information:

18,000 runners
Register at Piccadilly Hotel, collect running bibs and baggage labels to deposit clothing (no valuables) on baggage buses – displaying initial letter of surname.
2 starting positions. Blue – men who have run a marathon before. Red – women and 'first time' men.
Enter Greenwich Park by St Mary's Gate – check bar codes at Olivetti Marquee.

Overseas runners must obtain permission from own governing body.
All seek medical advice.
Increased number of rubbish skips.
Traffic restrictions lifted after 4½ hours.
Each mile signposted. Digital clocks along route.
Water every odd mile and sugar/salt drinks/first aid after every even mile.
p.m. – official awards ceremony at Inigo Jones Church.
Results published in *Running*.

This is how one student turned this information into a cheerful and informative letter. She did not add any information but slanted the material to get the right tone. Her own 'additions', which make the letter sound personal as well as informative, are underlined.

Kate Beckinsale

THE GILLETTE LONDON MARATHON 1983

1.

Dear Competitor,

I must begin by welcoming you to the Gillette London Marathon 1983. As Race Director, I am delighted to see so many of you taking part. But, with 18,000 runners, and the majority amateur runners, I must ensure that information concerning security, safety and the route itself has been fully understood.

You will shortly be registering at the Piccadilly Hotel where you will exchange your registration cards for official numbered running bibs. You will also collect numbered baggage labels, which enable you to deposit any clothing, with the exclusion of valuables, on the numerous baggage buses provided. The appropriate bus is simply the one displaying the initial letter of your surname.

This year's race has two starting positions. The blue start, for men who have previously run a marathon, and the red start for women and 'first time' men. All competitors must enter Greenwich Park by St Mary's Gate and report to the Olivetti Marquee where your computer bar codes will be checked. The race begins at 9.30 a.m. on 8 April.

We do suggest lightweight, comfortable running attire, although fancy dress is permitted. All overseas runners must obtain permission from their own governing athletic body, and everyone should have sought medical advice. Proper running shoes are essential – tennis shoes are inadequate.

Last year, we received complaints concerning litter left in Greenwich Park. We hope that the increased number of rubbish skips and your co-operation will eliminate this problem.

The race can be delayed by unruly or unco-operative behaviour of competitors. We do hope that this year's race will go as planned and that everyone will remain calm and sensible throughout. After the scheduled four and a half running hours, traffic restrictions will be lifted, and vehicles permitted to run as usual.

Each mile of the race will be signposted and digital clocks positioned along the route. Water will be available at every odd mile and sugar and salt drinks and first aid at every even mile.

The official awards ceremony will take place at the Inigo Jones Church the same evening, 8 April, and the results published in *Running* magazine.

I look forward to seeing you all on 8 April.

Yours sincerely,

Ron Fitt

RACE DIRECTOR

Question 2 required you to use *all* the information you were given, not just the passage, and to slant it a different way – this time to write a newspaper article, where the tone would of course be quite different from that of a fairly formal letter. Again, your first step would be note-taking of all the relevant information from your three sources:

NOTES
Peter Blake, 30, local teacher.
PHAB local charity Physically Handicapped Able Bodied.
Mrs Morgan: warden.
Centre needs new reception area: aim that handicapped to man it themselves – need telephone at wheelchair height, electric typewriter, dictaphone.
Include Mrs Morgan's quote.

MAP
Route goes from Greenwich–Woolwich–Westminster–Lambeth.

PASSAGE
18,000 runners.
8 April.
Running magazine.
Marathon medal for those who completed.
Services provided.
Blue start for veterans.

You could have chosen other information for your article – this question is not so strictly defined as question 1. Using this information, this is what the same student wrote:

LOCAL TEACHER RUNS MARATHON – PHABULOUS!

£186 is now to benefit a local charity thanks to teacher, Peter Blake.

Blake, 30, who teaches in Chiswick Comprehensive School, W4, ran the Gillette London Marathon with 18,000 other runners in order to raise money for his favourite local cause, PHAB – Physically Handicapped Able Bodied. The 26-mile marathon, held on 8 April, ran from Greenwich, through Woolwich and Westminster, and finished in Lambeth.

Mrs Janet Morgan, the charity's warden, was delighted to receive the money. She said, 'There have been several problems due to lack of funds. The money has come at exactly the right time.' The centre has needed a new reception area, and there were plans to allow the handicapped to man this new area. But without Mr Blake's money, the essential equipment has existed merely as a dream. Now, a new, push button telephone has been installed at wheelchair height, as has an electric typewriter, which is easy to use as it needs only a very light touch. The final amendment to the centre is a dictaphone with foot pedal and elbow switch for easy use.

Mr Blake also received a marathon medal as a prize for finishing the course and his achievements were published in *Running* magazine earlier this month. His time was 3 hours, 54 minutes.

Mrs Morgan says, 'This will enable the handicapped people here to do a real job and save us money.'

Mr Blake was very pleased with the work that has been able to take place due to his achievements. It was his first marathon but he was in training for five months in order to be fit enough to participate. He found it tough going but declared that all the services provided – the water, salt drinks and first aid from the gallant St John's Ambulance brigade – were a marvellous support. 'You felt you were being helped along.'

Will he be taking part next year? 'Definitely,' says Mr Blake, 'but I'll be at the blue start – for veterans – instead of with a bunch of women!'

The pun in the headline is very appropriate to a local paper. In fact, she stresses the 'local' interest throughout, keeping strictly to the rubric. The interview quotations are used throughout to lend the article a personal, informal tone, and the article ends on a suitably firm note. The two requirements of this kind of question – that of using relevant information and of adopting the correct tone – have been satisfied.

3. Talking and Listening

TALKING

Speech is our way of communicating in everyday life. We spend a very large part of our lives talking and listening. We may be arguing with a brother, making a speech in the debating society or telling a friend what we did at the weekend, but we are constantly thinking out what we need to say and organizing our sentences to suit the situation.

So it is quite appropriate that your GCSE English examiners should attach so much importance to your talking and listening skills. So much so, that you will need to obtain a Grade 5 in Oral English to pass GCSE English. This minimum grade won't represent a very high standard of achievement, though, so remember how important being able to communicate successfully is, in any job you can think of, and aim as high as you can. Use your English lessons partly as a time when you can become a more effective oral communicator. Don't just think of 'writing' as what is taught in English lessons. Every time a teacher asks you a question and you reply, you are exercising your Oral English skills.

The Oral English course, whichever group is setting your examination, is marked on 100 per cent continuous assessment and your teacher will be assessing your work throughout, within very strict guidelines laid down by the GCSE examiners. You will find that assessment goes on throughout the two-year course and the process may be continuing without your even being aware of it. Very often, you will be told when you are to be assessed for a specific oral activity but your grade will not simply be a result of how well you performed in the formal situations set up by the teacher. For instance, if a book you have been reading in class sparks off an interesting and fruitful discussion, the teacher may well take your contribution into consideration of your overall grade. If you consistently show enjoyment and interest in general discussions in your English lessons, this will certainly have a positive effect on your final grade. So, just as much as with your writing and reading, there are no cut and dried 'results' to be achieved. You should be concerned with your own personal progress over the two years. Don't look around constantly and compare yourself with others but concentrate on doing your best according to your own abilities. No one can ask for more, and your teacher knows that not everybody finds talking a very easy skill to master. You have plenty of time to find your feet – and your voice!

Over the two years, you will need to demonstrate your ability to communicate orally in a variety of different situations and for different purposes, so the teacher should give you many opportunities to talk and discuss in the classroom. The possible activities are numerous. Most of them, however, fall into two categories: when you are being formally assessed for this part of the examination, you will find that you are either involved in a *discussion*, or you are giving an *individual formal talk* to an audience. You should aim at becoming equally at ease in either situation although both types of communication may not come naturally to you.

Let's have a look, first, at how you could develop and improve your discursive skills.

Discussions

Quite a large percentage of your final grade will be accounted for by your participation in discussions. You could be assessed at any time, although you will usually be told in advance when assessment is taking place. There are different types of discussion, so we'll take group discussion, first, where you will be discussing a specific topic or issue with three or four other people.

The topic may be given to you, or you may choose it yourselves, depending on the exact activity the teacher has chosen for you. You could find yourselves discussing the pros and cons of school uniform, deciding how best to organize a trip to a local beauty spot, or even trying to interpret a poem together. You won't be in front of an audience – a discussion is not a performance. You will find that the teacher will be listening and watching you to see how well the group is getting on.

There are certain things you should try to do, and others you should avoid in a group discussion. Let's have a look at them:

DO

Introduce your points clearly.

Add to the points others are
  making.

Challenge or question what's
  being said.

Be aware of others in the
  group.

Listen to others.

Respond to the flow of the
  discussion.

Use personal examples and
  illustrations.

Speak clearly, so that you can
  be heard easily.

DON'T

Talk continually, over other
  group members.

Keep making the same point.

Sidetrack the discussion.

Be argumentative or aggressive.

Sit grumpy and silent.

Fail to listen.

Interrupt others.

Mumble.

It will help, of course, if you have had time to think about your task
beforehand. If you have, do use that time, perhaps to do a little research, but
certainly to prepare one or two points that you would like to make. Preparing
for an oral assessment is 'homework', just as much as a written assignment.

Interviews

There is another type of discussion on which you may be assessed, and that is
one in which you are involved in discussion with only one other person – your
teacher, a rôle-play interview with another student, or a genuine interview
when you are finding out something, perhaps for a written assignment.

Obviously, in this kind of one-to-one situation, you need to be particularly
attentive to the other person. Follow up comments, respond to what they say,
question, keep things moving. Don't ever answer with just 'yes' or 'no', and
don't ask questions which only allow this limited reply. Give the other person
an opportunity to talk, as well as you.

An interview with your teacher may well be part of your coursework
assessment. Your teacher may want to talk to you about a favourite subject or
hobby of yours, to see how well you can express yourself about something
that is very familiar to you. Some of you will find yourselves much more at

home in such a situation than in a group discussion, so you should use this opportunity to shine. Relax, listen carefully to what the teacher is saying, make sure you are answering the questions fully, speak clearly and audibly, and make eye contact, so that it seems you are actually talking to *someone*, not just a disembodied voice.

In a rôle-play interview, when one of a pair of students is an 'interviewer', the other the 'interviewee', you will need to prepare yourselves for either rôle in advance, deciding what you would answer in reply to certain questions, or preparing a list of thoughtful questions to ask. The rules are the same, though: listen, keep things moving on, make eye contact, respond to the discussion (don't just let it degenerate into a list of questions), speak clearly.

You might well find it helpful to watch very carefully when you see a TV chat-show interview or a more formal interview with a politician or public figure on the news. Ask yourself: Is the interviewer following up what the interviewee is saying? How probing are the questions? Is the interviewee answering fully? Is he speaking clearly? Is what he is saying interesting?

Watching others will help you to improve your own skills.

Giving a Talk

You're on your own, here! There may be a number of occasions during your course when you'll be required to stand up in front of the rest of the class and speak for a particular purpose. You may be asked to make a speech presenting a certain point of view, or in a debate, to tell a story, give instructions, or even introduce a passage which you are reading aloud. Whatever the precise nature of your assignment, the guidelines are the same, and there are really no excuses for not doing well. You will have plenty of time for preparation, the choice of subject matter will be very much up to you, and you won't have to worry about whether you are saying too much or too little, as in a discussion.

So, here are some dos and don'ts for giving a talk:

DO	*DON'T*
Plan your talk very carefully.	Skimp on preparation.
Keep the outline of the talk clear and simple.	Arrive on the day with muddled notes.

Be logical.
Know your subject inside out.
Use examples and illustrations
   to back up arguments.
Think 'audience awareness': make
   eye contact, look up often.
Speak clearly, slowly and
   audibly.
Relax and be natural.

Say things like 'Oh, and I
   forgot to say earlier . . .'
Ignore your audience.
Keep your eyes fixed on your
   notes.
Try to bluff if you're asked a
   difficult question, and you
   can't think of an answer.
Mumble.

Rôle-play

You may find that rôle-play has quite a regular place in your English lessons. It is an activity that both students and teachers enjoy, as it is an excellent way of demonstrating skill in understanding and imagination as well as oral proficiency.

Many teachers use rôle-play as a way of helping you to understand characters in a book you are studying in class, or to see complex moral dilemmas and social problems from different points of view. For instance, you might be asked to get into pairs and 'become' two characters from one of your GCSE English Literature books. You might discuss the events of the book from your (i.e. the characters') different points of view. Or, you might take the parts of a parent and a child: the child asks an awkward question and the parent tries to explain.

Both activities require an ability to 'step into someone else's shoes' and see things from their point of view. This is indeed a valuable life-skill to acquire: if you learn to understand others, you will find your enjoyment of life will improve tenfold. It won't just make any job you might do easier and more pleasant, it will make your social relationships happier, too. In many ways, rôle-play could be one of the most important things you ever do in an English lesson.

It's not that easy, though. You need to prepare carefully. Begin by imagining the person you're becoming very clearly: how they dress, speak, sit, where they live, what they do during the day and at the weekends. Then, try to imagine how these factors might make them *think*. You will be trying to convey through what you say and how you say it the processes of thought going on in that person's mind. Don't think of it as acting: you *are* the person for the few minutes you are being assessed, so you respond to what your partner is saying from that point of view, not your own.

Rôle-play also involves an awareness of what the GCSE examiners call register. This is the *way* you speak to different people, rather like tone in writing. For instance, suppose you had to explain something to your mother, then the same thing to your baby sister. Obviously, the language you would use, and your tone of voice, would be totally different in each situation. You would also cut out certain things that a child couldn't possibly understand. The examiners call this 'talking in different registers' and they consider it very important.

Am I Making Myself Clear?

This is a question you should be asking yourself constantly. No matter how good the content of your Oral English work, you won't get anywhere if you don't concentrate on how you present it. After all, this is an *Oral* English examination.

Don't worry about your accent. This is not an elocution examination, and you won't be expected to speak standard BBC English. The most important questions to ask yourself are:

1. Can I be heard all around the room? Or, by the other members of the group?
2. Am I varying the tone of my voice?
3. Or is it consistently too high or low?
4. Or very flat and monotonous?
5. Am I rushing what I'm saying, so it sounds blurred?
6. Do *I* sound interested in what I'm saying?
7. Am I aware of my audience? Or the other members of the group?
8. Or am I just looking at my notes or being completely selfish?
9. Am I listening attentively when others are speaking?
10. Am I constantly saying 'You know', 'I mean', 'Er', 'Well, I think'?

You are aiming at being easily heard and interesting to listen to. And, surely, this is what we would all like to be, throughout our lives.

The Oral English examination deserves a book of its own. These are only brief guidelines. To fill in the important details, you should read this book together with the 'Oral English' Passnote.

LISTENING

Aural Comprehension

Those of you who are taking the Midland Group (MEG) Scheme 1 examination will have to take an Aural paper accounting for 20 per cent of your marks. This is not to be confused with the Oral examination which you all have to take. This part of the examination concentrates on listening – one of the English skills the examiners want you to master.

You will be required to demonstrate the same kind of abilities in understanding, selecting relevant information and reorganizing material needed for the reading part of the exam. The big difference is that you will not just have written material in front of you – you will be hearing it, too. You will be asked to 'respond in writing to a recording of original spoken material, with attention to the manner, language and interaction of the speakers, as well as to its content'. In other words, to pay attention to *how* things are being said, as well as *what* is being said.

You will hear the recording twice; the first time you will just listen, the second time you will have both a transcript of the recording in front of you, and the question paper, and you will be able to take notes and annotate the transcript. Then, you will have fifty minutes to answer questions.

In many ways, this exercise is very similar to the Understanding papers we looked at earlier. You will know now that virtually anything can crop up there, and that is true of this part of the examination, too. The recording will almost certainly be a discussion, but it could be about anything at all, from nuclear war to trends in computer software. As in the Understanding section, you need to be ready for anything. It is also possible to work out a careful and consistent method of approaching this section which will enable you to tackle the questions with confidence.

What Are Listening Skills?

You may feel that there isn't anything very special about listening – you may also feel that it can hardly be described as a skill. However, if you think of any conversation you've had recently, you will probably find that you can only remember snatches of it, in no particular order. You may also find that other people will remember completely different parts of the same conversation, and to them it may have been an entirely different experience. In fact, we very rarely listen attentively and fully: we have one ear on the TV, our eyes on our homework and the other ear tuned in to our sister's telephone conversation. We are not really very good at concentrating. This examination paper is asking you to do just that, and it's not easy.

To gain high marks in this paper, you need to:

1. Understand fully the *content* of the recording.
2. Be aware of the *implications* of what is said.
3. Be attentive to the different tones of voice and to the mood of the discussion.
4. Be able to see the different positions the participants are taking in the discussion.
5. Select relevant material from the recording.
6. Reorganize that material for a specific purpose.
7. Write your answers in clear, logical, fluent and correct English.

Let's see how you can fulfil all these demands by going through the whole process from beginning to end.

The First Presentation

You are sitting in the examination room, waiting for the teacher to put the cassette on. The room is absolutely silent. Breathe deeply to relax yourself, close your eyes and empty your mind of everything – the lost pen, the dog's bad ear, your mother's bad temper, your friend's bad mood – and imagine a blank wall. The people in the recording will step out in front of it and start to speak, and you are going to listen to them.

During the first presentation, try to follow the main points of the discussion or conversation, and to come to some awareness of the conclusions reached. Ask yourself the following questions:

1. What are they talking about?
2. How many people are speaking?
3. Do they hold different views?
4. Do they sound angry? sarcastic? sad? kind? concerned? flippant?
5. Is there one speaker more dominant than the rest?
6. Can I begin to imagine what they must look like?
7. Are any conclusions reached at the end?

By the end of the first presentation you should have a *general* idea of the content of the recording and a *general* picture of the people taking part. Remember that you can check the *content* on the transcript. The most important thing to do while you are listening is to try to respond to the various people taking part – their different, perhaps conflicting, views and attitudes.

The Second Presentation

Before the recording is played for the second time, you will be able to read through the transcript and the questions. Use this time well. You will be able to listen to the second recording with an eye to answering the questions, so make yourself fully aware of what you are being asked. The examining groups have said that 'The questions will require candidates to respond in a variety of ways, both to what is said and the way in which it is said', so you will need to be well prepared for a wide range of questions.

While the recording is being played for the second time, you will be able to make notes on the transcript, keeping the question paper open. You should write brief notes to help you to answer the questions, underlining the relevant points and perhaps writing 'angry voice' or 'irritated' or 'she laughed here' on the paper to help you remember *how* something was said. A number of the questions will test that you have responded to people's moods and to their tones of voice, so you need to be very attentive to this aspect of the recording. You should make as many notes as possible on *how* things are said – you won't be able to remember people's voices, even after a few minutes, but you do have the transcript to help you with the content.

After the second presentation is over, you will have three minutes of silence to complete your note-making – just scribble down everything you can remember about people's tones, mood, and behaviour, that you think may be relevant in the answers. You can always discard anything you don't need.

You now have fifty minutes to answer a number of questions. You should refer both to the transcript and to your notes on tone and the general attitudes of the speakers. You will need to reorganize material very carefully and remember, again, to get rid of any irrelevant material. Use the same method you would use in an Understanding examination paper. Select relevant material for your answer and rearrange the points to be made. Then write your answer in full sentences, paying attention to grammar, spelling and punctuation. Don't rush and don't panic. Leave five minutes at the end for a read-through to check that you have completed all the questions and that your writing is accurate and fluent.

Now, let's have a look at a possible transcript and questions, and think how it could be successfully tackled.

Specimen Paper 1 – Aural (1 hour)

A transcript of a recording of spoken material is provided, with accompanying specimen questions.

The total marks for the specimen paper will be adjusted to the percentage allocated in the syllabus (20%).

The rubric for the examination paper will be as follows:

Instructions to candidates:

1 *You are about to hear an extract from a radio programme about factory-farming.*
  First you will hear the interviewer, next Mrs Cleal, who objects to factory-farming, and then Mr Flower, a farmer who supports that system.

2 *The recording will be played* **twice**: *the first time for listening and the second time for note making.*

3 *When you have heard the recording for the first time you will be allowed to open this question paper and read the questions. You will be given three minutes for this and then the record will be played again.*

4 *As you listen to the recording for the second time, you should make notes on the separate sheet of paper provided. After the second playing you will be allowed two minutes to complete your note making.*

5 *Attempt* **all** *questions, and write your answers in the spaces provided. You will be allowed 35 minutes in which to write your answers.*

INTERVIEWER: Well, we are in the calf-rearing house which is a low building about the size of half a tennis court. It's divided into four pens and here in front of us, in a typical pen, are eight young Friesian calves. They are taken away from the cows as soon as they are born, reared here on an artificial milk substitute which is always available to them and they have hay and they have underfloor heating and a wire mesh section for dunging. Now, Mrs Cleal, what are your objections to rearing calves in this method?

MRS CLEAL: A poor baby calf two days old crying for its mother. These little calves standing on hot concrete with just a thin layer of sawdust, you can see through the sawdust on the floor, they have no bedding – the straw is for them to eat, and it's standing up in a container here. And I am so sad at heart to see these poor creatures here.

FARMER: Now these calves are being reared automatically. They have hay . . .

MRS CLEAL: To eat.

FARMER: . . . a concentrate and the milk in front of them all the time. The environment is controlled in here at sixty-five. They never get the wind or the rain on them – if they were outside today these calves would be looking very sick indeed.

MRS CLEAL: They would not.

FARMER: As it is they are looking very bright . . .

MRS CLEAL: They are not looking bright.

FARMER: They are standing up here and from a farming point of view they are growing and doing extremely well.

INTERVIEWER: How long will they be reared in this building, to what stage?

FARMER: They will be in here for twelve weeks.

MRS CLEAL: They have never seen their mothers, they've been taken away at birth and standing on hot concrete, they have never had a gallop in the pastures and they have never had any natural life whatsoever.

FARMER: Well, they say that what you never had you never miss.

MRS CLEAL: That is not true, they have instincts and they have the way which God made them and you must not deprive them of all their God-given rights in this world.

FARMER: If these calves were put outside at the moment, they'd wonder where on earth they were.

MRS CLEAL: They would know.

FARMER: In the pouring rain they would be very miserable.

MRS CLEAL: They would now because of what you've done to them. Well, you've deprived them of their mothers.

INTERVIEWER: Let's go now on into the cow house and see their mothers and see the conditions in which they live and the dairy and the way they're milked. Here in this cow-shed it's a great covered yard about the size of three tennis courts. There are stands for sixty cows, a central passage where they go for feeding where silage is brought to them on a conveyor belt. They go in next door to the parlour for milking, and come back to their separate standings for sleeping and eating. Mrs Cleal, what is it you object to about this system?

MRS CLEAL: I want all of you to know that what I have seen today must never be forgotten. These are concrete walls, there are iron bars to keep each cow in its single pen. The floors are covered with dung, there is no straw here for them to lie on. I have seen the way they are to be fed automatically, they will never go outside this place, they go next door for milking, you see they are milk machines.

FARMER: These cows are held in this covered yard, particularly through the winter. They do go out in the summer although there are plans to keep cattle in all the year round. They are fed from a tower silo which holds the grass from the fields where it is brought in and then mechanically unloaded and delivered to the cows so they've got feed in front of them all the time. Where they lie is covered with sawdust and they have what is termed as cubicles which allows the cows to go in and lie there whenever they want. If you want milk for your children, somehow we've got to produce it. Are you willing to pay more for your food? If we are to go back to the method that you want us to do, we have got to charge you a lot more.

INTERVIEWER: Let us get the balance right between the cost of food production and the method of producing that food. Mr Flower suggests that he has got to produce his milk this way to make it an economic proposition for him and for the average housewife.

Would you be willing to pay a little more money for milk produced on free range, shall we call it?

MRS CLEAL: I think that if everyone could see what I am seeing now, they would never touch another drop of milk ever again because it's too big a price. Never mind the money, it's too big a price to pay in cruelty and misery for these living creatures.

FARMER: Last year world food production did not go up at all and yet there were seventy million more mouths to feed in the world. And unless more food is produced somehow or other in the world in the next ten years, in the next decade, there is going to be a lot of starvation.

MRS CLEAL: You aren't worrying about feeding the world, you're worrying about making big profits by exploiting the poor wretched animals and birds and the gullible public and I shall go on until every woman in this country knows what you are proposing to do and we will boycott the lot even if we have to be vegetarians.

1 Taking your information from what you have listened to, write a list of what you would see
   (a) in the calf-rearing house: (4)
   (b) in the cow house.   (4)
2 In the interview different points of view are heard about what is sometimes called 'factory farming'.

(a) Briefly express in your own words **one** of the criticisms made by Mrs Cleal and the farmer's reply to it. (4)

(b) Forgetting your own views on factory farming, say which of the two speakers you think presented his or her case the more effectively. Give your reasons. (4)

3 Basing your ideas on what you have heard, write part of a debating speech **either** for or against 'factory farming'. You should write approximately 100–150 words. (9)

Total Marks (25)

(MEG GCSE English Specimen Paper 1986)

Questions 1(a) and 1(b) test your ability to select relevant information from the transcript and to present it clearly. Your answer to 1(a) would include the following points to achieve full marks:

Low building, fifty feet long.
Four pens, each containing eight Friesian calves.
Concrete floor, sprinkled with sawdust.
Hay in containers in front of calves.
Milk available in troughs.
Wire mesh behind for dung.

And for 1(b):

Six times bigger than calf-rearing house.
Cubicles for sixty cows, enclosed by iron bars.
Concrete walls and floors.
Dung and sawdust on floor.
Central aisle for feeding.
Silage brought in on conveyor belt.

You can see that the points have been rearranged to make them seem more logical, and you would also need to make sure that your tone was completely informative and factual – there would be no place for any emotion in this answer.

Question 2(a) tested your ability to understand Mrs Cleal's arguments on factory farming. You might have picked the following criticism, and included these points:

Criticism relevant to both calf-rearing and milk production: *unnatural* environment. Hot concrete, no bedding, bars. No exposure to elements. Unable to follow natural instincts. Imprisonment.

Reply: calves and cows not used to anything else and would not adapt to 'natural' environment. Protected from elements – 'pouring rain'. As far as production is concerned, the animals are more efficient.

It would be very tempting, here, to include irrelevant details. Note that there are only *four* marks allocated – two for the criticism, two for the reply. So, you would be making approximately four points for the full marks. You would also need to make sure that you didn't quote from the transcript – it must be put into your own words.

Question 2(b) also carries four marks. Here, the key words are 'forgetting your own views'. In other words, look at the transcript and observe the tone and attitudes of the speakers, and draw conclusions without being prejudiced by your own views. You would need to have *listened* to this discussion to answer this question adequately.

In this kind of answer, you would need to look at how many good, solid points each speaker made, rather than emotional appeals. You would also need to look at how calm and collected they remained in discussion. Remember that emotionalism, hysteria and loss of temper create a very bad impression in discussions. Your answer would be based on these impressions.

The final question requires you to present a form of directed writing. Here, you would be using what you had heard and not adding your own ideas. You would also need to make sure that you were finding your own voice. It would be very easy to end up sounding just like Mrs Cleal or the farmer. All the points would need to be put in your own words and given a personal tone. You should not repeat phrases from the recording.

You might include the following points, bearing in mind that the allocation of marks is nine – probably five or six points for content, and three or four further marks for how successfully you put foward your argument:

For	*Against*
Constant food and warmth.	Discomfort of sheds.
Animals protected from elements.	Deprivation of natural instincts.
Efficient food-production method.	People would willingly pay more if aware of realities of methods.
Cheaper than traditional methods.	Exploitation of those who can't defend themselves (animals).
Modern methods help deal with greater demand.	Farmers out for fat profits.

A Final Reminder

In the Aural Comprehension paper:

1. Listen very carefully to the speakers' voices: note their different tones and attitudes.
2. Make extensive notes.
3. Select and rearrange your material carefully.
4. Use your own words.
5. Write in clear, accurate English.

4. *Your Coursework Folder*

All of you, without exception, will have to put together a coursework folder which will account for some percentage of your final mark. It could be as little as 20 per cent for some students studying for the Welsh examination and as much as 100 per cent for others all over the country. Think of your folder and your examination as making up a complete exhibition of your skills in written English. As we have seen, the courses have been designed so that you will get the opportunity to try out all kinds of different ways of writing, and to read and respond to a wide variety of literary and non-literary material. You need only think back to chapters 1 and 2 to realize just how wide the range of possible written and reading assignments is, and your coursework folder should do justice to that range. The examining groups do give you some guidance as to the *kinds* of writing they expect to see in your folder, but it is up to you and your teacher to ensure that you really do take note of that guidance.

HOW MANY PIECES OF COURSEWORK DO I NEED FOR MY FOLDER?

To remind yourself of exactly what you should be doing for your coursework folder, have a look at the information below:

LEAG

Written English: Paper 1: Teacher-assessed coursework   50 per cent
and either
Paper 2: Examination paper: Understanding
and Response   50 per cent

or

            Paper 3: Teacher-assessed coursework   50 per cent

Paper 1 Expression: 'Five units of work (400–500 words) to demonstrate a range of kinds of writing', *One* written under classroom supervision, *one* demonstrating 'discussion, argument or transactional writing' and *one* demonstrating 'narrative, descriptive or personal writing'.

Paper 3 Understanding and Response: 'five units of work (400–500 words) to demonstrate understanding of, and response to, close reading', *one* written under classroom supervision. The folder should 'show evidence of reading and informed response to a variety of texts', and evidence of reading one completely literary text.

                         (LEAG English Syllabus for GCSE 1988)

MEG

Syllabus A English (with Aural)

Scheme 1	Paper 1: (Aural)	20 per cent
	Paper 2 (Examination): (Directed writing and continuous writing)	50 per cent
	Paper 3: (Coursework)	30 per cent
Scheme 2	Paper 1: (Aural)	20 per cent
	Coursework	80 per cent
Scheme 3	Coursework	100 per cent

Scheme 1: Four units of work including *one* piece of personal, descriptive or narrative writing, *one* piece of argumentative or informative writing, *two* pieces showing response to reading during the course (and one of these must show evidence of reading of a whole text).

Scheme 2: Eight units of work, including *two* written 'under controlled conditions showing the candidate's ability to understand what he or she has read', *one* personal, descriptive or narrative essay, *one* argumentative or informative essay, and *two* pieces showing response to reading during the course (as for Scheme 1). The other two pieces would be further examples of these types of writing, or pieces 'illustrating the candidate's other strengths'.

Scheme 3: Ten units, including '*two* written under controlled conditions, *one* showing the candidate's ability to understand what he or she has heard and *one* showing the ability to understand what he or she has read', *one* personal, descriptive or narrative essay, *one* argumentative or informative essay, and *two* showing response to reading during the course (as for Schemes 1 and 2). *Two* of these pieces must be written under classroom supervision, in timed conditions. The further assignments are up to the candidate, as for Schemes 1 and 2.

(MEG Syllabuses for GCSE English 1989)

NEA

Syllabus A	Understanding/Expression paper	50 per cent
	Coursework	50 per cent
Syllabus B	Coursework	100 per cent

Syllabus A: five units, including *one* piece illustrating the understanding of non-literary material, which must be written in controlled conditions, *two* pieces where the teacher has given a specific assignment, and *two* pieces decided by the candidate. *One* of these pieces must show 'evidence of the reading of one whole work of literature'.

Syllabus B: ten units, including *one* illustrating reading and response to a whole literary text, *one* piece of argumentative/persuasive writing, *one* piece of factual writing, *one* illustrating response to reading on the course. The other assignments can be further examples of the above, or other units demonstrating different skills. *One* of the assignments must be written in timed conditions, under classroom supervision.

(NEA Syllabuses for 1989)

Southern Examining Group

Syllabus A	Paper 1: Understanding/Directed writing	25 per cent
	Paper 2: Directed writing	25 per cent
	Coursework	50 per cent
Syllabus B	Coursework	100 per cent

Syllabus A: six pieces of work (of 2,500 words approximately), including *one* piece of descriptive writing, *one* piece of narrative writing, *one* piece of creative writing, and *two* written in response to literature read during the course. *Syllabus B*: twelve units (of 400 words or more) of the following types: expressive/imaginative; discursive/argumentative; explanatory/instrumental; (at least two of each of these); and *four* based on material read during the course (*two* literary, *two* non-literary). *Three* of these assignments should be written under classroom supervision, in timed conditions.

(Southern Examining Group Syllabuses for 1988)

Welsh Joint Education Committee

Either	Paper 1: Understanding/Expression	50 per cent
	and Coursework A	50 per cent
or	Paper 1	50 per cent
	Paper 2: Expressive/Factual	30 per cent
	and Coursework B	20 per cent

Coursework A: candidates should assemble *eight* pieces of work covering a range of writing skills. Final assessment will be based on the best five pieces of work, chosen to satisfy the following requirements: *two* pieces of writing of an imaginative nature; *two* pieces of 'argumentative persuasive writing'; *one* piece of 'informative writing'.
Coursework B: two units, 'employing argument or expressing opinion'.

(Welsh Joint Education Committee Syllabus for 1988)

Of course, you should check these requirements with your teacher, to make sure that you know exactly where you are. Don't forget that this is very definitely a two-year course. All the groups stress that this folder should represent your 'best' work, but many examiners expect to see work from your second *and* first years of the course. You should check this point with your teacher. You can't just sit back for a year, and produce eight pieces of work at the last minute. Be very strict with yourself: make sure that you are keeping up with all your homework assignments and that your teacher doesn't have huge gaps in the mark-book beside your name. You and your teacher will decide which of the assignments you have completed over the two years represents your 'best' work and during the spring term before your final assessment, you will sort them out for the folder. It is worth bearing in mind, throughout the course, that *any* piece of work could be included, so give everything you do your best shot. There is no point in wasting opportunities to do well.

Let's consider what the contents of an ideal coursework folder might be, so that you have a clearer idea of what you are working towards.

A BIT OF VARIETY

We'll take two examples: first of all, a student taking the NEA Syllabus A, Paper 1 and 50 per cent coursework option; then, a student taking MEG Scheme 3 (100 per cent coursework). In both cases, I have shown you which of the 'assessment objectives' that the examiners talk about, would be fulfilled in each assignment.

NEA

If you look back to the NEA's requirements, you will see that they ask for *five* pieces of coursework: *one* demonstrating understanding of non-literary material, written under controlled conditions; *two* assignments set by the teacher; and *two* where the subject matter is largely decided by the candidate. One of the five pieces must demonstrate 'evidence of the reading of one whole work of literature'.

The written examination paper will also test both understanding and response and skills and expressive writing, so the coursework, as you might expect, complements the written paper. The two taken together will show your abilities in a very wide range of areas.

A student taking this option might include the following items in his or her coursework folder:

1. A paper written in timed conditions, in class, under the teacher's supervision. This might consist of answers to the questions about the tables, including the report-writing, shown on pp. 104–108. This unit of work demonstrates the following skills:

a. Understanding and conveying information.
b. Understanding, ordering and presenting facts.
c. Evaluation of information; the selection of what is relevant to specific purposes.

2. Answers to a set of questions, such as that shown on pp. 80–83, to demonstrate understanding of, and response to, poetry. This unit of work demonstrates the ability to:
  a. Evaluate information and select what is relevant to specific purposes.
  b. Recognize implicit meanings and attitudes.
  c. Articulate experience and express what is felt and what is imagined.

3. An essay entitled: 'Is Vivisection Really Necessary', including photographs, information and statistics relevant to the essay and gathered by the candidate. This unit of work demonstrates the ability to:
  a. Order and present facts, ideas and opinions.
  b. Express what is felt.

4. An essay entitled: 'The Tree-house'. A personal and autobiographical account of a much-loved place. This unit demonstrates the ability to articulate experience and express what is felt and what is imagined.

5. A continuation of a novel, read in class as part of the GCSE English Literature course. This unit reflects appreciation of a complete text read on the course and demonstrates the ability to:
  a. Evaluate information and select what is relevant to specific purposes.
  b. Recognize implicit meaning and attitudes.
  c. Articulate experience and express what is felt and what is imagined.

MEG

MEG Scheme 3 requires you to submit *ten* pieces of coursework: *one* 'showing the candidate's ability to understand what he or she has heard and *one* showing the ability to understand what he or she has read'; *one* piece of expressive writing; *one* piece of argumentative or informative writing; *two* units written in response to the candidate's reading during the course. A coursework folder might include *all five* of the units described above and:

6. An aural 'understanding and response' exercise, such as that illustrated on pp. 126–130. This unit tests the ability to:

   a. Understand and convey information.
   b. Understand, order and present facts.
   c. Evaluate information and select what is relevant to specific purposes.
7. An imaginary letter, written by a character in one of the books studied during the course, telling a friend, or another character, about the events of the book. It would be written from that character's point of view. This unit would illustrate the same skills as No. 5.
8. A further expressive essay: a story entitled 'Never Say Die'. This unit would illustrate the same skills as No. 4.
9. A newspaper article about the conditions at a local mini-zoo. This unit would demonstrate the same skills as No. 3, and journalistic persuasive skills.
10. A survey, compiled at school, about students' eating habits. This would include statistics in the form of a bar chart or graph, and a 'report' detailing the conclusions to be drawn from the survey. This unit would demonstrate similar skills to those in 3 and 9.

   To an examiner, both of these folders would look very thoughtfully put together. All the requirements have been fulfilled and there is evidence of a wide variety of written work on the course.

Could I Rewrite Any of My Work for My Folder?

You may discuss your work with your teacher, re-draft and change material before you write your final draft. However, when you have written a final draft, and the teacher has marked it, you should not make any further alterations. The piece of work should go into your coursework folder as it stands. It goes without saying that any piece of work which you submit must be entirely your own work, marked by your teacher.

What Should My Folder Look Like?

Think of how much you can learn from your first impression of a person – their clothes, the way they speak, their general appearance – and remember that the same thing applies to your work. A well-organized, neat, clean folder will suggest an orderly mind – and the reverse is true, too!

Your coursework should be put into a clean, plain manila folder, and be on lined A4 paper. On the cover of the folder, you should write your name, your candidate number and the number of your centre (your teacher will tell you these). Each piece of work should be clean and carefully written, and not full of crossings-out or ink-blots. They should all be very clearly dated, and the title of the assignment should indicate its precise nature. For instance, if a piece of work has been completed in timed conditions, this must be obvious. You should also say how much time has been spent in class discussing or preparing the assignment. For example, if you had spent one lesson reading a poem in preparation for answering questions on it, you might put: 'The poem was read in class and we discussed its meaning and how we felt about it. We were then given these questions to complete for homework.' If you have not made a note of this at the time, don't worry too much, as your teacher will have kept records so you can check with him or her, and attach a little note giving these details. The work should also show what the examiners call 'evidence of having been marked by the teacher'. It is no good putting in work at the last minute, unmarked. Such pieces of work would be discounted.

Separate each piece of work distinctly, perhaps using paper or card dividers. When you have chosen all your assignments, arrange them in what seems to you an appropriate order, to emphasize their variety, and number the pages. Then write a clear Table of Contents to insert at the front of the folder, giving page numbers. So, when the examiner, or your teacher, opens the folder, he or she will see at once what to expect and will have been given the impression of careful presentation. If you like, you may include a short introduction to your folder, explaining why you chose to include these pieces of work.

Aim at making things as easy as possible for your teacher and your examiners. If your work looks orderly and careful, your table of contents is accurate and helpful, and you have complied with all the examining group's requirements, you will already have gone a long way towards doing well. On the other hand, if your units of work are dog-eared and full of chocolate smudges and your writing looks untidy and careless, or if the table of contents is cramped, unclear or inaccurate, you won't be creating a very good first impression. There is no substitute for excellence, but you *can* help excellence along by making it look neat and tidy!

Using Your Reading

All the examination groups want to see evidence of your reading in your coursework folder.

Many of you will find that much of the work you do for English Literature, whether or not you are taking an English Literature GCSE, will be closely linked with your Language work. The GCSE examiners look on English and English Literature as all part of the same course anyway, so it is quite appropriate that so much importance should be attached to reading.

There are many coursework assignments arising from your reading which you could include in your folder. I have suggested some possibilities below. You can probably think of many others.

1. An examination of one of the incidents, or even the central issue, of a book, in the form of a newspaper report.
2. A diary written by one of the book's central characters, describing his or her feelings.
3. A letter written from one character to another, justifying his or her actions in the book.
4. A dialogue between two characters in the book, where they look back on and discuss the book's events.
5. An imaginary letter from you to a friend, where you record your impressions of the characters in a book as if you have just met them (see pp. 94–5).
6. A continuation of a book, or play.
7. A trial, where the central character of a book is brought to account for his or her actions, and found guilty or not guilty.
8. A 'genre transformation', that is, a poem written about the same subject, characters and themes as a book or play, or a short story or play based on the events of a poem.
9. A TV or radio interview with one of the book's central characters.
10. A short story about the events leading up to the beginning of the book.

You can discuss other possibilities with your teacher.

If you are also taking English Literature GCSE, you must be very careful not to repeat material in your Literature and English folders. You may include pieces of work on the same books, but the material must not overlap.

I have included one such coursework assignment here, as an example. This was written by a student in the first year of the GCSE course. It is a newspaper account of the events in Graham Greene's short story 'The Destructors'. Note that she has used interviews to create a sense of immediacy and reality in the report.

WORMSLEY GAZETTE

THURSDAY OCTOBER 26th.

HOUSE BUJLT BY WREN DESTROYED BY KJDS

Yesterday, No 3, the only surviving house on Northwood Terrace after the first Blitz, was totally destroyed by a gang of youths.

The house belonged to a Mr Thomas, and was built by Sir Christopher Wren. Jt was a beautiful, historic house, and was one of the land marks of Wormsley Common. **Gang** (sub-heading)

Jt was destroyed by a small gang of youths, who call themselves "The Wormsley Common gang". The leader, and the brains behind the operation, is Trevor, who is called T by the gang. Trevor's father is a former architect, and says he has no idea why Trevor would do such a thing.

Experts say that the gang must have destroyed all the furniture, and things inside the house first, and then pulled the walls down from outside – a difficult job. **Weekend**

The gang must have known that Mr Thomas was going away for Bank holiday weekend and decided to destroy his house then.

Jn a statement to the police, Mr Thomas said "Well, J decided it was too cold when J was away and so J came back home. As J was walking back along the Common, when J heard a whistle and a child shouting my name. Jt seemed to come from my own garden. Then a boy ran up to me and told me one of his friends had used my loo, which is in the garden, ✓ and had got stuck in it. He told me to hurry along in case he suffocated, J said "Rubbish", but he dragged me along to the back and told me to climb over the wall. He snatched my bag and put it on the other side, so J had to climb over. Somebody was shouting from the loo, or near it anyway. When we arrived, J pulled hard on the door, and as it opened, J was pushed in. **sub-heading: Sausages**

J was locked in, and kept there all night, but they gave me a blanket and some buns and sausage rolls, probably to keep me quiet. One boy said something about me not being comfortable in my house, and that set me thinking, but there was nothing J could do, so J just sat in that loo until next morning, when J heard a man in the car park. J shouted, and he came and let me out. Sub-heading: Rubble

When J saw that pile of rubble, that pile of my house, J just couldn't believe it, J shouted "Where's my house". Then that man, the man who had unlocked the door, laughed, he laughed at what had happened.

All J want to know is why they did it. That boy who asked to see my house, why did he destroy it? Why did he hate me or it so much? Orders

Trevor also made a statement to the police: "J didn't hate the house, it was a beautiful house, but J had to

destroy it. The gang didn't understand, they were just following orders. Jt was me. J just wanted to destroy it, destroy it so there was nothing left. Jt was nothing personal, Mr Thomas, really, J don't hate you or anything, J don't hate your house either, but J hated it's beauty. J'm sorry Mr Thomas, but J had to do it".

Jt has been agreed that Trevor should be sent to a Psycho. analyst, and Mr Thomas is staying with relatives until further arrangements can be made

Report by Ellen Taylor

A Very Fair Assessment

The most obvious feature of coursework is its flexibility. As it is largely up to you and your teacher what goes into your folder, there is no reason at all why it should not show you at your best. It is not like an examination, where so many things can go wrong on the day.

So do yourself justice! Put all your enjoyment and satisfaction in this subject into your folder, remembering that what you have enjoyed doing and made an effort with will usually be a pleasure to read, even if it isn't 'perfect'.

5. Examination Technique

Most of you probably feel that you've done far too many examinations already. It is certainly true that between the ages of five and twenty-one, you will spend a large amount of time thinking about, working towards, and revising for, timed examinations.

Ideally, though, you should not look at examinations as something you work for frantically at the last minute, then forget about. In fact, all your GCSE courses have been specially designed to *avoid* this approach to examinations. If a public examination rather than work undertaken in timed conditions in class is part of your GCSE English course, it should be seen as a logical and natural progression from the work you have done throughout the two years. It should not be a goal towards which you are working (for many of you, coursework will account for a far higher percentage of marks than the examination). Worse still – it should not be a terrible trauma that has you shaking in your shoes for the two years leading up to it. A balanced, practical approach to examinations, and a willingness to prepare calmly and carefully without panicking, is what you should be aiming at – not an irrational fear or unnatural obsession with success.

WHY DO WE NEED EXAMINATIONS?

You may well ask! It is something that examiners themselves have been debating for years, and attitudes to public examinations differ widely. Most people agree that an examination is one of the best ways of making an *objective* test of your knowledge and abilities. Your achievement in public examinations and in timed conditions on your course will be set beside your achievements under more leisurely, relaxed conditions. The two together give the people who are assessing you a full, rounded picture of *you* as a student.

You should also remember that working in strictly controlled, timed conditions – producing results within a limited period – is in itself a valuable skill. There are many occasions, whatever course you pursue in life, when you will be called upon to do just that. It is worth being prepared to face such challenges.

WHAT'S THE BEST LONG-TERM APPROACH TO MY EXAMINATION?

For GCSE English, you will find yourself sitting either a Writing paper or a Reading and Understanding paper, or both. The examination will test the skills we have discussed in the Reading and Writing chapters of this book, and you will already be familiar from those chapters with the kind of question that might be asked.

By the time you sit your examination(s) you should have had plenty of practice in all different kinds of reading and writing for your coursework. So, if you have pulled out all the stops, never being satisfied with less than your best, you will have a very good idea of your capabilities. You should also make sure that you have attempted some of your assignments in strictly controlled timed conditions, have learned to discipline yourself and have seen past examination papers, or similar exercises, well before you sit your own examination. Your teacher will organize this for you, so that when you go into your examination you will already be confident that you have done it before; you should know your own weaknesses, and try to avoid being defeated by them.

HOW CAN I BE SURE OF DOING MY BEST ON THE DAY?

Some people just seem to have the knack of doing well in examinations: irritating, but true. It is a great mistake to compare your own achievements to those of others under any circumstances, as everyone is an individual, but this is particularly true of examinations. Don't just dismiss yourself as an examination candidate because you may have found them difficult at the age of seven. Good examination candidates are born *and* made. While there will always be those people who breeze through, there are also those who transform themselves through hard work and self-discipline from very ordinary examinees to outstanding ones.

Doing well largely depends on technique, and this can be learnt. The techniques to acquire for English are slightly different for the Writing and Reading and Understanding papers, but there are certain things to remember and take note of which are common to both papers, so we'll begin by looking at those.

Ten Things to Remember in the Examination Room

1. **Don't panic**.
2. **Concentrate** hard.
3. **Don't be put off** by a large amount of material to master: some Reading and Understanding papers are very long.
4. **Read the instructions** slowly and carefully and make sure you follow them.
5. **Note how many marks** are allocated to each question.
6. **Always write in full sentences**.
7. If you need to make **rough notes**, make sure they are **neat, clear and organized**. Draw a diagonal line through any rough work.
8. Keep an eye on your **spelling, grammar, punctuation** and general **presentation**. Write clearly and legibly.
9. **Time yourself** carefully and very strictly.
10. Leave yourself five minutes at the end to do a **final check**.

Let's have a look at these pointers in more detail:

1. **Don't panic**. A cool head is something we all admire, and it can mean the difference between success and failure in the examination room. It may be that at first sight the exam paper might look as if it has been written in gibberish. Often, you can be so tense that things seem to make no sense at all. This feeling of panic is quite natural, and will subside almost immediately if you just tell yourself quietly that this paper is nothing unusual; you have seen it all before; you are well prepared, and determined to do your best; it may take a few minutes to make sense of what is in front of you, but you will soon be writing away quite fluently.

2. **Concentrate** hard. Concentration will help to chase away any feelings of panic. Don't gaze around to see how your friends are reacting to the paper. Keep your mind fixed firmly on the pages in front of you. Push out any distracting thoughts. You have a very short time to do justice to your abilities so it is in your interest to dismiss from your mind anything that might stop you doing well.

3. **Don't be put off** by a large amount of material to master: some Reading and Understanding papers are very long. Reading the instructions or rubric on the examination paper is without doubt one of the most crucial parts of the examination. The examiners have designed these rubrics to give you as many clues as possible about how to do well. So *don't rush*. Read your instructions slowly and carefully, underlining the important parts, whether it's the directions for a Reading and Understanding exercise or the list of possible essays on a Writing paper. Never, ever, just glance over them once, assuming that you have understood fully at a brief reading. Read them *three times*: then, repeat to yourself in your mind what you have to do – this will help you to 'fix it' mentally and you will be far less likely to make mistakes.

4. **Read the instructions** slowly and carefully and make sure you follow them. You may find yourself wading through a number of pages of material before you get to, or are given, your questions. Don't rush and don't waste time, but work through methodically, coming to a thorough understanding of what you have been given. Make notes, underline important words and phrases and remember all you learnt from chapter 2. Again, don't panic.

5. **Note how many marks** are allocated to each question. This may seem obvious, but it is very easy to plunge into answering a question without taking too much notice of how many marks it is worth. So, you may end up, if you are not careful, giving a ten-line answer to a question worth two marks, and a two-line answer to a question worth ten marks. Remember that if a question is worth five marks, the examiners are probably expecting you to give an answer containing about five points. The amount of marks allocated also tells you how long your answer should be. Clearly, a question only worth two marks would require a very short, straightforward answer.

6. **Always write in full sentences**. Again, this may seem a very obvious point, but under examination conditions some people do degenerate into a kind of shorthand. Don't let it happen to you. Write in full,

complete sentences, even when answering a very short question.

7. If you need to make **rough notes**, make sure they are **neat, clear and organized**. Draw a diagonal line through any rough work. Your notes don't need to be neat for the examiner, who will probably only glance at them. They need to be neat for *you*, as you are the one who will have to decipher and reorganize them. So space them out well, and make sure you can read them.

8. Keep an eye on your **spelling, grammar, punctuation** and general **presentation**. Write clearly and legibly. All the things we will discuss in the Basic Skills section can tend to slip a bit in timed conditions. Somehow, it is much harder to think of the difference between 'their' and 'there' in an examination room. Sentences turn into page-long marathons and commas disappear altogether, or appear instead of full stops, and paragraphs are nonexistent. Year after year, examiners express their surprise at the fact that even after repeated warnings from teachers, and constant reminders on the papers themselves, candidates still neglect these basic skills. Writing a good essay when your spelling, punctuation and handwriting are all appalling is like trying to paint the *Mona Lisa* with a decorator's brush: it just can't be done.

9. **Time yourself** carefully and very strictly. When you are working through your paper, you should constantly be aware of time passing. Don't waste valuable minutes gazing into space and don't write desperately, either, trying to cover as many sheets of paper as possible. If your paper is two hours long, and has two sections carrying equal marks, spend the same amount of time on each section unless you are told otherwise. Don't leave yourself too much to rush through at the end. If there is quite a long question at the end of a Reading and Understanding paper, leave yourself sufficient time to do justice to it. You should find that you finish just in time to check through your paper. If you have twenty minutes or so to spare, you have either missed something out or failed to answer several questions adequately.

10. Leave yourself five minutes at the end to do a **final check**. Examiners can spot an unchecked paper a mile away. It's the one with no full stops or capital letters, no page numbers at the top and littered with spelling mistakes. The last five minutes in the examination room should be spent reading through your work looking for spelling mistakes, bad punctuation and poor grammar. You should also check that every question is clearly numbered (if you're doing an essay paper, make sure you indicate

clearly which essay you have attempted) and that the pages are clearly numbered 1–10, so that if they do become separated, it will be easy to put them back in order. Your name should be on each sheet of paper. This is also the time to check that you have answered every question and have crossed out your rough work. It is a vital five minutes and leaving out this final process is a sure way of losing marks.

PUTTING THEORIES INTO PRACTICE

Bearing all these pointers in mind, let's now have a look at two extracts from GCSE exam papers from the point of view of examination technique. We'll start with a list of possible essays for a Writing examination. A number of you, those who have to do a Writing as well as an Understanding and Response paper, will have to make a choice of essay from a list of titles, and produce something in quite a short time. There are certain things that you can do and other things to avoid, which will help you to produce an essay which genuinely does represent your best efforts.

First of all, look at the rubric carefully: 'Paper 2 (1½ hours). Answer *both* questions. You are advised to spend some time planning your answer in each case.'

The fact that the examiners have mentioned planning shows you that you would be very unwise to leave this out. You will be expected to give in some rough work. Now on to question 1, the essay section: 'Write on *one* of the following topics. You are advised to spend about an hour on this question (40 marks). The quality of your writing is more important than its length, but as a general rule your work should cover 2 or 3 sides of the pages in your answer book.'

The examiners are being very helpful here. Two or three sides is not really very much, and this should alert you again to the fact that, more than anything else, they seem to want your essay to be thoughtful, well planned, coherent and compact. So, you would probably be wise to spend ten minutes or so planning very carefully (look back at chapter 1). Your first step, however, is choosing your title and it is all too easy to pick a loser. So how do you avoid it? Here are the titles – but you should avoid glancing at them very briefly and frantically, then concluding, 'They're boring – I can't do any of them'. Read each title carefully, opening your mind for a moment to its possibilities, and underline the ones that strike you at once as good options:

(a) My Mum or My Dad
(b) The joys or the miseries of a winter's afternoon on the school field.
(c) Marathon
(d) Describe a crowded beach. As you watch, a thunderstorm breaks and the holidaymakers run for shelter. Describe the events as they happen and conclude by describing the deserted beach.
(e) 'I never felt so ashamed in my life!' Write about a personal experience – perhaps a joke that misfired or a time when you unthinkingly hurt a loved one – which ended with you feeling very guilty and ashamed.
(f) Write imaginatively in response to *one* of the pictures.
(g) Disaster Area.

(Welsh Joint Education Committee Specimen Paper 1988)

These are the sort of thoughts that should be passing through your mind as you consider each title separately (you will already know from your two years of coursework where your strengths and weaknesses as a writer lie):

(a) This is a good choice for someone who can write about people they know well with affection, amusement, and observant detail. Have you done particularly well in the type of exercise which involves this kind of honest, amusing, observant approach? If so, this is for you – unless, of course, you have done *exactly* the same essay before. If you have, avoid this title at all costs. The phrases and ideas which got you high marks on your course will sound stale and uninspiring if you produce them again. There is no mistaking the sparkling nature of fresh and original work.

(b) Again, you will be writing from your own experience here. If you chose this title, your main task would be to avoid sounding like everyone else in your year group. They will have the same range of experiences as you, so it would be especially difficult to produce something original. However, if you are good at creating particular kinds of atmosphere, can draw successful thumbnail character sketches, and have an accurate ear for dialogue, you might enjoy writing this essay.

(c) This title suggests a number of possible approaches, but there would need to be a definite story-line, unlike (a) and (b). If you have discovered a talent as a storyteller, and know that you aren't likely to fall into cliché and turn out the same sort of thing as everybody else, this might suit you. You would work out your plot and characters using the methods we discussed back in chapter 1. Your main enemy would be the clock; it is very difficult indeed to write a convincing and compact story in under an hour. You need to be very confident. It would also help your scene-scetting if you had been to a marathon, or knew someone who had prepared for one. It would be unwise to try to fit the title to a story more loosely connected with it – such as the struggles of a handicapped or disadvantaged person to be successful. Such attempts very often backfire as, however good the essay, the examiners will penalize you very heavily for being irrelevant. When in doubt, always go for the most obvious interpretation of the essay title.

(d) This is an absolute gift question for those of you who have been in this very situation. The essay would need to be packed with closely observed details about the place *and* the people, and you would need to create 'before' and 'after' atmospheres successfully. Those of you who enjoy writing about what you can see and hear, and have a good sense of place, would excel in this one. You could certainly still do the essay even if you had not had this precise experience. You would just add your experience of a crowded beach to your experience of a thunderstorm, and let your imagination do the rest.

(e) You would need to be able to think immediately of an experience which has stuck in your mind – perhaps something very recent – which still has the power to bring the colour to your cheeks. The essay would have to be filled with your embarrassment for it to work successfully, so that the reader could understand how you felt. You would also need to distance yourself from the experience, too, so that the essay would not become an indulgent confession.

(f) The picture would just *have* to appeal to your imagination. The skills involved in this kind of essay are essentially descriptive, although you can also write a story in response to a picture. It would be a great temptation to be irrelevant, so you should not even attempt this essay unless you know you have considerable control over yourself as a writer.

(g) This title could be a disaster area for you if you allowed yourself to get carried away. You would get no marks at all for an essay drawing its inspiration from American disaster films, or even from your reading. As very few of you will have first-hand experience of a disaster area, it might be wise to avoid this title unless you are a very imaginative, controlled writer. However, the phrase is so often applied to *people* who are generally accident-prone or incompetent, that in this case it would be quite appropriate to take a slightly different angle and write an essay based on the character of a person who might be described as a 'disaster area'. Such an essay would come to life if you knew someone like that, and, again, if you were an observant person, good at recording thoughts and feelings about others.

Once you have made your choice, plan your essay carefully, and keep an eye on the time. Don't leave yourself with too many ends to tie up, and keep on checking your plan to make sure you are not moving away from the title. Leave five minutes to check through the essay at the end of the examination.

Finally, we'll have a look again at the rubric to an Understanding and Response question which we have already examined in some detail, this time from the point of view of examination technique. Read through the rubric on pp. 112–13 once more.

First of all, you would need to be very calm while reading through the large amount of material you are given, and to resist the temptation to look at the questions too early. Note that both questions carry equal marks and therefore require equal time and effort. You are told *not* to use invented material, to *base* your answers on the facts, but you are also reminded to use your own words and to reorganize your material. You should always bear such advice in mind while writing your answers.

The rubrics for both questions 1 and 2 are very detailed. There is a lot of help for you, here.

You are given details of the beginning, end, and the date of the letter, so all you have to do is make sure that the layout is good, and not cramped. You are told that the purpose of the letter is to inform and advise, and the tone should be welcoming but also firm. You would need to ensure that all the information was presented in a logical way, and that you did not include any irrelevant information. You would also have to take care to avoid the letter turning into a mere catalogue.

On the second question you are given detailed advice as to layout. You are clearly expected to make your answer look as much like a newspaper article as possible, using a headline and even subheadings. You can safely assume that you are also expected to adopt the general tone of a local newspaper – playing up the 'local' part of the story – and you are also told that your audience is 'general'. So, you would need to write in a simple, clear and direct style to appeal to everyone. Much more reorganization of information would be needed than for the first question. Your main priority would be making your answer look and sound as much as possible like a newspaper article. You are also reminded to use *all three* sources of information – something that is easily forgotten. It is a common mistake to concentrate on just one of your sources in this kind of question, and this can cost you a great deal of marks.

A FINAL WORD ON EXAMINATIONS

Examiners don't enjoy reading poor scripts and take no pleasure in failing candidates. They want their task to be as much fun as possible so they are actively looking for good things about your examination scripts, and are not, contrary to popular belief, trying to catch you out.

It should be clear from this chapter that there is no great mystique involved in doing well in examinations, and that the instructions are there not to baffle, but to help you. So take them in your stride. If you have kept up with the work throughout your course, and have made yourself fully aware of your strengths and weaknesses, they don't need to present a major problem.

6. Basic Skills

WHAT IS A SENTENCE?

A sentence is a group of words which can stand by themselves and make full grammatical sense. The first word begins with a capital letter, and every sentence ends with a full stop. In between these it must have a finite verb. What this means will become clear as you read the sections below.

The Parts of a Sentence

We can divide a sentence up into three basic components. Knowing what these are will help you to recognize when you are writing 'real' sentences, and when you are not.

i. *The subject*: the name given to the noun or pronoun about which or whom a statement is being made, e.g.:

Ben is my neighbour.   Ben = Subject.
He plays the guitar.   He = Subject. The pronoun 'he'
                                   stands for the noun.

ii. *The Predicate*: The name given to the part of the sentence which tells you about the subject, e.g.:

Ben is *my neighbour*.   my neighbour = Predicate, as it
                                   tells you about Ben.

iii. *Finite Verb*: the finite verb in a sentence has a subject, like 'Ben' and can form a tense, e.g. Ben is, was, has been, playing the guitar.

Non-finite forms of the verb can't stand by themselves and make sense. They are:

a. The infinitive: to play the guitar
b. The present participle: playing the guitar
c. The past participle: played the guitar
d. The verbal noun: guitar playing

Examples

a. play the guitar – is not a sentence
b. Ben playing the guitar – is not a sentence
c. Played Bob Dylan – is not a sentence
d. His playing – is not a sentence

Now, *this* is a sentence:

Ben	plays	the guitar
↓	↓	
Subject	Verb	Predicate

None of the groups of words a–d make sense on their own, so they are not sentences. When you are writing, constantly ask yourself if your sentences are 'real' – if they make grammatical sense in themselves. Don't fall into the trap of not making it clear to the examiner that you know what a sentence is. For instance, in a descriptive essay, you might be tempted to write loosely and impressionistically, like this: 'A clear, golden day. Sun on the lake, and the birds wheeling overhead. Hardly a ripple on the water.' There isn't a full grammatical sentence in sight! Or, at a tense moment in a story, you could, in your excitement, produce something like this: 'A locked door. The sound of a baby crying inside. Steps leading upwards.'

This kind of writing can very easily look slipshod. It is allowable to use such a technique very sparingly indeed, but ideally you should aim at writing complete sentences all the time.

WHAT IS A PARAGRAPH?

A new paragraph in a piece of prose begins with a line slightly indented from the margin. Beginning a new paragraph is a way of telling your reader that you are moving on to a new idea or a different angle on the subject you are writing about.

You should learn to paragraph efficiently as it is another way, like writing good, clear sentences, of helping your readers to understand what you are trying to say.

Arranging your work into paragraphs helps to give it structure. When you are planning a piece of writing, think about the area you want to cover in each paragraph and make sure that each one follows on to the next. Generally speaking, when you have arranged everything you want to say into a logical order, you should find yourself paragraphing quite naturally.

When you forget to paragraph – and a number of people do in the tense atmosphere of the examination room – you are badly weakening the effect of your writing. An ability to arrange your work into coherent and connected paragraphs is essential both for success in the GCSE English examination and for your future career.

Remember to vary the length of your paragraphs, as you would vary the length of your sentences. Aim at creating different effects in different paragraphs. Keep those readers interested!

WHAT IS PUNCTUATION?

Accurate punctuation, like good paragraphing and well-constructed sentences, helps your readers to understand what you are trying to say. When you punctuate, you are also indicating how you would want your writing to be read out loud – it is a guide for your readers. Effective punctuation is essential to make your meaning completely clear. Inaccurate punctuation obscures your meaning and can lead to ambiguities and confusion.

We'll look at all the main punctuation marks in this section: full stops, commas, semi-colons, question and exclamation marks, hyphens, dashes and brackets. We'll also look at the rules for direct speech, the apostrophe 's', and capitalization.

The Full Stop (.)

You put a full stop when you have reached the end of your sentence. The word which follows always begins with a capital letter. It sounds simple enough, but it is easy to forget to put them in or to replace them with commas when you are in a hurry. So don't rush your work, and put your full stops in as you go along. Remember that a full stop indicates quite a sharp pause in your writing, so use it when you want your reader to take a deep breath.

Have a look at the following sentence:
> She ran down the path, he was waiting for her, they caught the bus together.

It sounds clumsy and inexact when you read it aloud. However,
> She ran down the path. He was waiting for her. They caught the bus together.

sounds reasonable. Even better would be:
> She ran down the path, where he was waiting for her, and they caught the bus together.

which sounds accurate and well-paced.

The comma (,)

This is probably the most widely used and abused punctuation mark in existence. It should be used to:

a. divide a sentence up into different parts to make it easier to understand.
   Examples:
   i.   He had been driving steadily for an hour, with no other car on the road.
   ii. In front walked an old man, stooping his weight on to a stick.
   iii. Leaving him standing there, we went up to the top room.
   iv. Judy had never owned a doll, never heard of Cinderella, never played at any game.
b. separate items in a list ('and' replaces the comma between the last two items).
   Example:
   i.   . . . at last we go on to a real country road again with windmills, rickyards, milestones, farmers' wagons, scents of old hay, swinging signs and horse troughs.
c. mark off words and groups of words, in pairs.

Examples:

i. I walked quietly on, talking softly to the growling dog, till I was ten paces away.

ii. Since father died, sir, I've gone out to work.

iii. Did she though, really, Charley?

As you can see, the pauses make the meaning of the sentence clearer.

Commas are often but not always used after these link words:

after	before	unless
although	but	until
and	for	when
as	if	whether
because	since	while

You have to use your common sense to judge when a pause is needed in the sentence. Link words can also appear at the beginning of a sentence. Have a look at these two examples:

> One evening, *when* I was about fourteen, I was walking down the side of a field . . .

> *Before* going on up into the blue hills, Tomas Gomez stopped for gasoline at the lonely station.

Note that the following words are *not* link words, so don't use them to join different parts of a sentence together:

actually	so
however	then
in fact	therefore
in this way	thus
nevertheless	yet
on the other hand	

You can, of course, use these words at the beginning of your sentences.

The Exclamation Mark (!) and the Question Mark (?)

Both of these punctuation marks come at the end of a sentence and replace the full stop. You use the exclamation mark at the end of an exclamation, order or command. The question mark appears only at the end of a direct question. Never use both together and only use one exclamation mark at a time.

Examples:

Where are you going?
What an awful day!
     Remember that it is very easy to leave question marks out, so do be careful.

The Semi-colon (;)

This is useful, but very difficult to use correctly, so beware. It indicates a pause midway between a comma and a full stop. It always links two related ideas, complete in themselves. Before using a semi-colon, ask yourself: Would my writing be clearer if I used a full stop here? If the answer is 'yes', avoid the semi-colon. Don't use it unless you are completely confident.

Example:

The rain pattered on the roof; outside, she could see her sister walking through the wet grass.

The Colon (:)

This always tells your readers that something is coming next. It may introduce a list of words or phrases, quotations, explanations of the first part of the sentence or, very occasionally, direct speech. When it introduces a list of phrases, semi-colons are used to separate them.
     Here are some examples of its use.

a. I began to feel a new sensation, as well as fear: loneliness (explanation of first part of the sentence, introduced by colon).
b. The old man said: 'My greetings to your father' (direct speech introduced by colon).
c. Hamlet's most famous speech begins: 'To be or not to be: that is the question' (quotation, introduced by colon).
d. 'We took with us on our picnic: cakes, sandwiches, biscuits and cans of fizzy drink' (a list of words introduced by a colon; note the use of the

comma rather than the semi-colon, as it is a list of words, not phrases or groups of words).

e. She had more than her fair share of faults: apparently boundless laziness; an inflated sense of her own importance; an inability to see reason and a rotten temper (a list of phrases introduced by a colon; note the use of the semi-colon to separate the phrases).

The Hyphen (-)

This is used either to indicate that a word has been split in two at the end of a line, or when a 'compound word' has been made out of two or more separate words, such as 'breakfast-room' or 'son-in-law'. Try to avoid dividing words between lines wherever possible in your writing. If you must, then split them up in syllables, rather than in mid-syllable: neigh/bour, not neighbo/ur, for instance.

The Dash (–)

You can use a dash to indicate, at the end of the sentence, that what follows is a climax, anti-climax, or perhaps a witty or surprise ending to a paragraph or essay. It makes the reader draw breath before the next word, in anticipation.

You can also use it to indicate a remark made aside, or an interruption to the flow of the sentence, as in this example:

I had no thought that night – none, I am quite sure – of what was soon to happen to me.

An 'aside' made in this way is often called a 'parenthesis'.

Beware of over-using dashes, as this can be a very lazy way of punctuating your work. Use them very occasionally, when you want to create a specific effect.

Brackets ( )

These are used for the same reasons as pairs of dashes and are also used to separate longer passages from the main flow of your writing:

I had no thought that night (none, I am quite sure) of what was soon to happen to me.

Direct Speech

There are certain rules for presenting the precise words which people are saying, in your writing. You must know these rules and observe them at all times.

You use *inverted commas* (quotation or speech marks) to indicate when someone is speaking and you must take great care over the punctuation of the sentence. Have a close look at these three examples:

1. He said, 'I'm fed up with this.'
    Note that the comma comes after 'said' and *before* the first speech mark. What is said begins with a capital letter and ends with a full stop, inside the speech marks.
2. 'I'm fed up with this,' he said.
    Note that the comma comes *inside* the second speech mark and that 'he' does *not* have a capital letter. That is because the complete sentence doesn't end until after 'said'.
3. 'Well,' he said, 'I'm fed up with this.'
    Note that the comma comes after 'Well' *inside* the speech mark and *after* 'said', *outside* the speech mark.

Remember to start a new paragraph for each new speaker.

Learn these examples, and by imitating the conventions used here you will be able to tackle writing your own dialogue with the minimum of difficulty.

Inverted commas are also used for: the titles of books, plays, poems, radio and TV programmes, newspapers, magazines, ships, and for shorter quotations.

The Apostrophe s ('s)

This causes more problems than any other form of punctuation. But it needn't, if you remember that it always indicates either possession or a letter or letters that have been left out.

When you attach 's to a word, it means that the next word or group of words belongs to it. You should be able to turn the phrase round to bring this relationship out more clearly, as in these examples:

Sarah's dress: the dress belonging to Sarah

Andrew's bedroom: the bedroom belonging to Andrew

The Government's proposals: the proposals belonging to the Government

You decide who or what is the owner and put an apostrophe at the end of that word followed by an s.

Problems arise when the word which owns something is a plural ending with an s. The rule is exactly the same: decide on the word that is doing the 'owning' and put the apostrophe after that word but *leave out the second s.* Look at these examples:

The bees' stings

The trains' wheels

and note that there are no apostrophes attached to either 'stings' or 'wheels' because the stings and wheels don't own anything. It is a very common error to throw in an apostrophe every time you see a suspicious-looking s. Keep the rules strictly in your mind, don't panic, and you will avoid this mistake.

What to do when the singular word that owns something ends with an s, as in 'jeans' or 'James':

There is no doubt that 'the jeans's zip' sounds clumsy; so use your common sense, get rid of the second s, and it becomes 'the jeans' zip', which sounds much better. Similarly, 'James's guitar' sounds reasonable, but 'James's sandwiches' sounds very awkward. You would keep the s before 'guitar' and get rid of it before 'sandwiches' – as in this case there are too many s sounds, so you can leave the apostrophe on its own.

Note that 'its' indicating possession *never* has an apostrophe:

The dog licked its paws.

However, apostrophes are also used when words have been shortened or when two words have been put together, with letters left out. Here, the apostrophe means 'something left out' and it always appears in the space where the letter or letters should be, for example:

it's: it is

isn't: is not

don't: do not

they're: they are

Try to shorten your words in this way only in quite informal writing or direct speech. This kind of informality would be unsuitable for, say, a discussion essay or report.

Capital Letters

A capital letter always begins a new sentence. You also use them for: places, names of people and pets, streets, rivers, mountains, entertainment events, teams, cinemas, ships, cars, aeroplanes, newspapers, books, films, TV programmes, plays, pop songs, the days of the week, the months of the year and titles, such as 'Lord'.

Remember that when you are addressing an individual, as in the sentence 'What shall I do, Mother?', you use a capital letter. When you are generalizing, it's 'mothers'. You write about 'prime ministers' in general but 'the Prime Minister made a speech'.

AGREEMENT

If your sentences are to make sense, you must observe the rules of 'agreement'. The subject of a sentence must agree with its verb, and the tenses of your verbs should be consistent. You will remember from chapter 1 that there are third-person and first-person ways of telling a story. If you use a third-person noun, you must use a third-person verb to agree with it. Let's have a look at the first-, second- and third-person words:

First: I, me, myself, my, mine   (singular)
we, us, ourselves, our, ours   (plural)
Second: you, yourself, you, yours   (singular)
you, yourselves, your, yours   (plural)
Third: he, him, himself, his   (singular)
she, her, herself, her, hers
it, itself, its
they, them, themselves, their, theirs   (plural)

These are also third-person words:

anybody	everyone	no one	something
anyone	everything	nothing	
anything	nobody	somebody	
everybody	none	someone	

and you should use singular third-person words to go with them – i.e., he, him, himself, etc. Use singular forms of the verb, too. This is the kind of thing you are trying to avoid:

Somebody went home with their satchels.

'Somebody' is a third-person singular word, so you must use the third-person singular possessive 'his' satchel, for agreement.

Possible Problems

This/that; these/those

'This' and 'that' are singular; 'these' and 'those' are plural. Avoid this kind of clumsiness:

These types of dog and those types of cat are pedigree.

In a case like this, it would be better to turn the sentence around completely, so that it sounds less awkward:

The following breeds of dog and cat are pedigree.

The verb 'to be'

Take extra care using the verb 'to be':

There were twenty people in the room.

plural   plural

The group of tourists is over there.

singular   singular

'Either . . . or' and 'neither . . . nor'

When 'or', 'either . . . or', 'neither . . . nor' join singular nouns or pronouns, a singular verb is needed and this verb agrees in person with the noun or pronoun nearest to it as in:

Mrs Jones or Mr Anderson is going to be there.

Neither the Headmaster nor the Deputy Head likes the idea.

Either he or you should go home.

Collective nouns

This is the name given to several persons or things of the same kind, regarded as a group, such as: crowd, class, committee. They are usually singular and are followed by a singular verb:

The class was in an uproar.

The committee was set up to deal with housing.

But sometimes it is necessary to use a plural verb, when we are using the collective noun to refer to a number of individuals performing different actions, e.g.:

The committee were all proposing different solutions.

The class were all involved in various activities to raise money.

Agreement of Tenses

All verbs have tenses: either past, present or future. When you use more than one verb in a sentence you must make sure that the tenses agree, as well as making sure that the subject and verb agree. The following sentence sounds wrong because the tenses do *not* agree:

I *went* to the barn, and *sit* down on the floor.

but both of these sentences are correct:

I went to the barn, and sat down on the floor.

I went to the barn, where I am now sitting on the floor.

Common sense is your best guide, here. If you are thinking carefully about what you're writing you will generally find that your tenses will come quite naturally. You must be consistent, and keep checking your work as you go along.

SPELLING

Don't ever be fooled into thinking that you can get through your GCSE – and through life – spelling badly, because you can't. It is true that some people just seem to be able to spell while others can't but if you are not one of life's natural good spellers you can't afford to sit back and do nothing about it.

The first thing you can do to tackle spelling difficulties is to check through this very long list, which contains most of the commonly mis-spelt words noticed by examiners and teachers. Write down all the words you can't spell, from this list, in a notebook, in groups of ten. Learn them systematically and test yourself, over a long period of time. As you work through the list, keep going back to test yourself on words you learnt days or weeks ago, as you need to give your brain time to store the words away in your long-term memory.

When you are doing a coursework assignment, and you want to use a word but are not sure how to spell it, *use your dictionary.* Then, learn the spelling at once, and enter the word in your notebook. You should get into the habit of entering any words which you have mis-spelt into this notebook. As you begin to spell words correctly, without having to think about them, tick them off and concentrate on the words which are still causing you problems.

absence	analysis	biscuit
accelerate	anxious	bodies
accept	appalled	bored
accepted	appalling	bought (buy)
accidentally	apparent	Britain
accommodation	approach	broken
achieve	arctic	brought (bring)
achievement	argument	buried
acquaintance	ascent	business
across	associate	camouflage
address	attach	category
adjacent	attempt	caterpillar
advantage	author	ceiling
advertisement	autumn	cellar
affair	awful	cemetery
affect (influence)	awkward	century
agreeable	bachelor	changeable
alcohol	banister	character
almost	beautiful	chimneys
already	because	choose
also	beginning	climbing
although	behaviour	clothes
altogether	being	college
always	believe	colour
amount	bicycle	comment

committee

competition

completely

conscience

conscious

corridor

countries

courageous

cries

cupboard

damaged

deceive

decided

definitely

delicately

dependent

describe

desperate

detach

deteriorate

develop

development

diary

difference

different

dilemma

dining-room

disappeared

disappoint

disastrous

discuss

discussed

disease

disregard

dissatisfied

distort

drawers

eagerly

easily

effect (result)

embarrass

embarrassment

emigrate

enrol

entered

enthral

equipped

eventually

everybody

everyone

exaggerate

except

excitement

exercise

exhilarating

existence

experience

extension

extremely

failure

favourite

February

fictitious

field

finally

finished

foreign

forestall

forty

friend

fulfil

furniture

gaol

gaping

gauge

glamorous

glamour

glimpse

goal

government

grateful

grieved

guarantee

guard

guest

gullible

haggard

handkerchief

handled

happened

harass

height

helpful

hoard (treasure)

holiday

honourable

hordes (crowds)

humorous

hypocrisy

icy

illegal

imitate

immediately

immensely

impertinent

incidentally

independent

ingenious

innocent

intelligent

interfere

interrupt

intrigue

irrelevant

irreparably

irritable

jealous

jewellery
keenness
knowledge
laboratory
labour
laid
language
leisure
library
lightning
likeable
listen
literature
loneliness
loser
lovable
magazine
magnificent
manoeuvre
mantelpiece
miniature
minutes
mischievous
momentous
monastery
muscles
museum
must have
mystery
necessary
neighbour
niece
ninety
noisy
noticeable
nuisance
obedient
obscene
occasion

occasional
occurred
occurrence
omitting
opportunities
ordinary
originally
paid
paper
parallel
pastime
people
perhaps
permanently
persistent
personally
picnicking
pigeon
pity
pleasant
possessive
practical
precaution
preferring
prejudice
presence
privilege
probably
procedure
proceed
procession
professional
programme
prominent
pursue
quarrelling
queue
quiet
quieter

receipt
received
recognize
recommend
reference
regrettable
relevant
remember
repetitive
responsibility
restaurant
rhyme
rhythm
safely
scandal
scene
scheming
secretary
seize
sentence
separate
sergeant
severely
Shakespeare
shining
shriek
silhouette
similar
sincerely
sizeable
skilful
smiling
soldier
solemn
something
souvenir
spiteful
squalor
stomach

stopped	tough	veterinary
stretched	tragedy	vicious
studying	travelling	Victorian
subtly	travels	view
succeed	treacherous	village
successful	tries	virtuous
superstitious	trolleys	weather
supplies	truly	Wednesday
suppose	tyranny	weird
sure	umbrella	whereas
surprise	unnatural	whether
suspicion	unnecessary	whining
suspicious	until	wondrous
technology	usually	woollen
telephone	utmost	worrying
temperature	valleys	would have
temporary	valuable	writing
tendency	vandalism	yacht
theatre	vapour	yield
tolerant	vegetable	

Spelling Rules

These are almost endless, and generally take too much time to understand and learn. Rather than learning a long list of rules, you would be better off reading as much as possible and noting the spellings of the words you are reading.

However, there are just a few rules which you should try to learn, as you will find them very helpful indeed.

1. ie and ei: 'i' before 'e', except after 'c' when the sound is 'ee': niece; believe; field; *but* ceiling; deceive.
   Exception: seize
   ei: not pronounced 'ee'; foreign; forfeit; feint; leisure; reign; skein; surfeit; veil; weir; weird.
2. -ful: when you make a compound word with 'full', or any word ending in 'll', the 'll' changes to a single: grateful; skilful; beautiful; fulfil.

When you make this word into an adverb ending in 'ly', then the 'lly' comes back: skilfully; gratefully. (Note that it's *not* 'ley'.)

3. -ly: to make an adverb (describing the verb), add 'ly' to the describing word: crossly; gruffly; anxiously.

   Exceptions: duly; truly; wholly.

   When the descriptive word ends in a consonant + 'le', change the 'e' to 'y': irritably; sensibly.

   When it ends in a consonant + 'y', change the 'y' to 'i' and add 'ly': icy: icily; racy: racily.

   When it ends in 'ic', add 'ally': cynically; ironically.

4. Plurals of words ending in 'y': When the word ends in a consonant + 'y', the 'y' changes to 'i' and is followed by 'es': country: countries.

   When the word ends in a vowel + 'y', add 's': valley: valleys.

   This rule also applies to the different forms of verbs such as: try: tries; fry: fries; *but:* say: says.

   The 'y' is always kept for the ending 'ing', to avoid the awkwardness of two 'i's together: marrying; trying.

Exceptions:	dry	drier	driest	drily	dryness
	gay	gayer	gayest	gaily	gaiety
	shy	shyer	shyest	shyly	shyness
	sly	slyer	slyest	slyly	slyness

5. -our: when 'our' comes at the end of a word, keep the 'u' when 'able' is added: honour: honourable.

   When 'ous' is added, drop the 'u': humour: humorous.

VOCABULARY

In the Writing chapter, we have already looked at how important your choice of words is in creating the desired effect in your writing. Regular, varied reading should help to build up your awareness of the kind of words you can use for different types of writing. Any unfamiliar words should be looked up at once in a dictionary, and you should aim at extending and widening your vocabulary – not just for G C S E English, but for your own interest. A wide, flexible vocabulary is something we all admire in writers and speakers and your teachers and examiners will be looking closely at the words you use.

So, choose your words with care. Avoid clichéd and overused buzz words. *Listen* to your writing: get rid of words that sound clumsy, awkward or ugly. Your writing should be good enough to read out loud, too.

What is Slang?

Slang is a kind of shorthand we all use in spoken English, but we should try to avoid it in written English unless we are reporting direct speech. Slang varies from decade to decade, so it dates easily. For instance, it was fashionable to refer to new trends as 'groovy' in the Sixties: I think we would all smile if we heard someone saying that, now. 'She's a bit thick' is a slangy version of 'she's not very intelligent'. Such colloquialisms are quite acceptable when you're writing dialogue, but nowhere else.

What is a Cliché?

A cliché is an overworked, overused word or phrase. You hear plenty of them on TV, so you should be able to recognize them. They are tired, stereotyped phrases used by people who are too lazy to think of anything original to say. The expressions may once have been distinctive, but their constant repetition has devalued them. Think of how boring the following sound: 'this day and age'; 'at this moment in time'; 'the wind of change'; 'at the end of the day', 'the generation gap'; 'in the wake of (the election etc.)'; 'the dream turned into a nightmare'. These phrases are dull, stale, and tired. So are many of the proverbs and idioms you might have come across, such as 'hitting the nail on the head' and 'toeing the line'.

Avoid this lazy and thoughtless type of expression. If you have something to say, think of your own fresh and original way of saying it. Don't borrow somebody else's words.

The following list should help you to see what to avoid in your writing. A number of these words have been singled out by examiners and teachers as some of the most objectionable words found in students' work:

a bad time	fantastic	nice
ace	firstly	O.K.
actually	freaked out	or whatever
a lot	get/got	really
amazing	good	serious
and so on	great	smashed (drunk)
awful	grotty	smashing
basically	hassle	sort of
brilliant	hopefully	thick (stupid)
chucked out	in this day and age	thing
cool	meaningful	traumatic
etc.	mega- (anything)	well
fabulous		

You can't write a good sentence without varied and appropriate vocabulary. So work at it – you will be rewarded by an increased enjoyment of your reading and writing.

Pieces marked by teacher — and
submitted to folder   139.
Table of contents

⊛   Short list of contents
explaining why certain pieces
were picked.

Writing || Reading + Understanding
Paper || Paper.

Q — Prospectus. Which board
have our classes allocated?

FOR THE BEST IN PAPERBACKS, LOOK FOR THE

In every corner of the world, on every subject under the sun, Penguin represents quality and variety – the very best in publishing today.

For complete information about books available from Penguin – including Pelicans, Puffins, Peregrines and Penguin Classics – and how to order them, write to us at the appropriate address below. Please note that for copyright reasons the selection of books varies from country to country.

In the United Kingdom: For a complete list of books available from Penguin in the U.K., please write to *Dept E.P., Penguin Books Ltd, Harmondsworth, Middlesex, UB7 0DA*

In the United States: For a complete list of books available from Penguin in the U.S., please write to *Dept BA, Penguin, 299 Murray Hill Parkway, East Rutherford, New Jersey 07073*

In Canada: For a complete list of books available from Penguin in Canada, please write to *Penguin Books Canada Ltd, 2801 John Street, Markham, Ontario L3R 1B4*

In Australia: For a complete list of books available from Penguin in Australia, please write to the *Marketing Department, Penguin Books Australia Ltd, P.O. Box 257, Ringwood, Victoria 3134*

In New Zealand: For a complete list of books available from Penguin in New Zealand, please write to the *Marketing Department, Penguin Books (NZ) Ltd, Private Bag, Takapuna, Auckland 9*

In India: For a complete list of books available from Penguin, please write to *Penguin Overseas Ltd, 706 Eros Apartments, 56 Nehru Place, New Delhi, 110019*

In Holland: For a complete list of books available from Penguin in Holland, please write to *Penguin Books Nederland B.V., Postbus 195, NL–1380 AD Weesp, Netherlands*

In Germany: For a complete list of books available from Penguin, please write to *Penguin Books Ltd, Friedrichstrasse 10 – 12, D–6000 Frankfurt Main 1, Federal Republic of Germany*

In Spain: For a complete list of books available from Penguin in Spain, please write to *Longman Penguin España, Calle San Nicolas 15, E–28013 Madrid, Spain*

FOR THE BEST IN PAPERBACKS, LOOK FOR THE

PENGUIN CLASSICS

Netochka Nezvanova Fyodor Dostoyevsky

Dostoyevsky's first book tells the story of 'Nameless Nobody' and introduces many of the themes and issues which will dominate his great
masterpieces.

Selections from the Carmina Burana A verse translation by David Parlett

The famous songs from the *Carmina Burana* (made into an oratorio by
Carl Orff) tell of lecherous monks and corrupt clerics, drinkers and
gamblers, and the fleeting pleasures of youth.

Fear and Trembling Søren Kierkegaard

A profound meditation on the nature of faith and submission to God's will
which examines with startling originality the story of Abraham and Isaac.

Selected Prose Charles Lamb

Lamb's famous essays (under the strange pseudonym of Elia) on anything
and everything have long been celebrated for their apparently innocent
charm; this major new edition allows readers to discover the darker and
more interesting aspects of Lamb.

The Picture of Dorian Gray Oscar Wilde

Wilde's superb and macabre novella, one of his supreme works, is
reprinted here with a masterly Introduction and valuable Notes by Peter
Ackroyd.

A Treatise of Human Nature David Hume

A universally acknowledged masterpiece by 'the greatest of all British
Philosophers' – A. J. Ayer

FOR THE BEST IN PAPERBACKS, LOOK FOR THE

PENGUIN CLASSICS

A Passage to India   E. M. Forster

Centred on the unresolved mystery in the Marabar Caves, Forster's great work provides the definitive evocation of the British Raj.

The Republic   Plato

The best-known of Plato's dialogues, *The Republic* is also one of the supreme masterpieces of Western philosophy whose influence cannot be overestimated.

The Life of Johnson   James Boswell

Perhaps the finest 'life' ever written, Boswell's *Johnson* captures for all time one of the most colourful and talented figures in English literary history.

Remembrance of Things Past (3 volumes)   Marcel Proust

This revised version by Terence Kilmartin of C. K. Scott Moncrieff's original translation has been universally acclaimed – available for the first time in paperback.

Metamorphoses   Ovid

A golden treasury of myths and legends which has proved a major influence on Western literature.

A Nietzsche Reader   Friedrich Nietzsche

A superb selection from all the major works of one of the greatest thinkers and writers in world literature, translated into clear, modern English.

Matthew Arnold	**Selected Prose**
Jane Austen	**Emma**
	Lady Susan, The Watsons, Sanditon
	Mansfield Park
	Northanger Abbey
	Persuasion
	Pride and Prejudice
	Sense and Sensibility
Anne Brontë	**The Tenant of Wildfell Hall**
Charlotte Brontë	**Jane Eyre**
	Shirley
	Villette
Emily Brontë	**Wuthering Heights**
Samuel Butler	**Erewhon**
	The Way of All Flesh
Thomas Carlyle	**Selected Writings**
Wilkie Collins	**The Moonstone**
	The Woman in White
Charles Darwin	**The Origin of Species**
Charles Dickens	**American Notes for General Circulation**
	Barnaby Rudge
	Bleak House
	The Christmas Books
	David Copperfield
	Dombey and Son
	Great Expectations
	Hard Times
	Little Dorrit
	Martin Chuzzlewit
	The Mystery of Edwin Drood
	Nicholas Nickleby
	The Old Curiosity Shop
	Oliver Twist
	Our Mutual Friend
	The Pickwick Papers
	Selected Short Fiction
	A Tale of Two Cities

FOR THE BEST IN PAPERBACKS, LOOK FOR THE

PENGUIN CLASSICS

Benjamin Disraeli	**Sybil**
George Eliot	**Adam Bede**
	Daniel Deronda
	Felix Holt
	Middlemarch
	The Mill on the Floss
	Romola
	Scenes of Clerical Life
	Silas Marner
Elizabeth Gaskell	**Cranford** and **Cousin Phillis**
	The Life of Charlotte Brontë
	Mary Barton
	North and South
	Wives and Daughters
Edward Gibbon	**The Decline and Fall of the Roman Empire**
George Gissing	**New Grub Street**
Edmund Gosse	**Father and Son**
Richard Jefferies	**Landscape with Figures**
Thomas Macaulay	**The History of England**
Henry Mayhew	**Selections from London Labour** and **The London Poor**
John Stuart Mill	**On Liberty**
William Morris	**News from Nowhere** and **Selected Writings and Designs**
Walter Pater	**Marius the Epicurean**
John Ruskin	**'Unto This Last' and Other Writings**
Sir Walter Scott	**Ivanhoe**
Robert Louis Stevenson	**Dr Jekyll and Mr Hyde**
William Makepeace Thackeray	**The History of Henry Esmond**
	Vanity Fair
Anthony Trollope	**Barchester Towers**
	Framley Parsonage
	Phineas Finn
	The Warden
Mrs Humphrey Ward	**Helbeck of Bannisdale**
Mary Wollstonecraft	**Vindication of the Rights of Woman**

FOR THE BEST IN PAPERBACKS, LOOK FOR THE 🐧

PENGUIN CLASSICS

Arnold Bennett	The Old Wives' Tale
Joseph Conrad	Heart of Darkness
	Nostromo
	The Secret Agent
	The Shadow-Line
	Under Western Eyes
E. M. Forster	Howard's End
	A Passage to India
	A Room With a View
	Where Angels Fear to Tread
Thomas Hardy	The Distracted Preacher and Other Tales
	Far From the Madding Crowd
	Jude the Obscure
	The Mayor of Casterbridge
	The Return of the Native
	Tess of the d'Urbervilles
	The Trumpet Major
	Under the Greenwood Tree
	The Woodlanders
Henry James	The Aspern Papers and The Turn of the Screw
	The Bostonians
	Daisy Miller
	The Europeans
	The Golden Bowl
	An International Episode and Other Stories
	Portrait of a Lady
	Roderick Hudson
	Washington Square
	What Maisie Knew
	The Wings of the Dove
D. H. Lawrence	The Complete Short Novels
	The Plumed Serpent
	The Rainbow
	Selected Short Stories
	Sons and Lovers
	The White Peacock
	Women in Love

PENGUIN CLASSICS

John Aubrey	**Brief Lives**
Francis Bacon	**The Essays**
James Boswell	**The Life of Johnson**
Sir Thomas Browne	**The Major Works**
John Bunyan	**The Pilgrim's Progress**
Edmund Burke	**Reflections on the Revolution in France**
Thomas de Quincey	**Confessions of an English Opium Eater**
	Recollections of the Lakes and the Lake Poets
Daniel Defoe	**A Journal of the Plague Year**
	Moll Flanders
	Robinson Crusoe
	Roxana
	A Tour Through the Whole Island of Great Britain
Henry Fielding	**Jonathan Wild**
	Joseph Andrews
	The History of Tom Jones
Oliver Goldsmith	**The Vicar of Wakefield**
William Hazlitt	**Selected Writings**
Thomas Hobbes	**Leviathan**
Samuel Johnson/	**A Journey to the Western Islands of**
James Boswell	**Scotland/The Journal of a Tour to the**
	Hebrides
Charles Lamb	**Selected Prose**
Samuel Richardson	**Clarissa**
	Pamela
Adam Smith	**The Wealth of Nations**
Tobias Smollet	**Humphry Clinker**
Richard Steele and	Selections from the **Tatler** and the **Spectator**
Joseph Addison	
Laurence Sterne	**The Life and Opinions of Tristram Shandy,**
	Gentleman
	A Sentimental Journey Through France and Italy
Jonathan Swift	**Gulliver's Travels**
Dorothy and William	**Home at Grasmere**
Wordsworth	

FOR THE BEST IN PAPERBACKS, LOOK FOR THE

PENGUIN PASSNOTES

This comprehensive series, designed to help O-level, GCSE and CSE students, includes:

SUBJECTS
Biology
Chemistry
Economics
English Language
Geography
Human Biology
Mathematics
Modern Mathematics
Modern World History
Narrative Poems
Nursing
Physics

SHAKESPEARE
As You Like It
Henry IV, Part I
Henry V
Julius Caesar
Macbeth
The Merchant of Venice
A Midsummer Night's Dream
Romeo and Juliet
Twelfth Night

LITERATURE
Arms and the Man
Cider With Rosie
Great Expectations
Jane Eyre
Kes
Lord of the Flies
A Man for All Seasons
The Mayor of Casterbridge
My Family and Other Animals
Pride and Prejudice
The Prologue to The Canterbury
    Tales
Pygmalion
Saint Joan
She Stoops to Conquer
Silas Marner
To Kill a Mockingbird
War of the Worlds
The Woman in White
Wuthering Heights